HEARING
the Voice of
GOD

Lisa Banados

Gazelle
PRESS

ISBN 1-58169-140-8
For Worldwide Distribution
Printed in the U.S.A.

Gazelle Press
PO Box 191540, Mobile, AL 36619

Table of Contents

Dedication

I dedicate this book
to my loving husband Rolando
who has stuck with me through thick and thin,
and who has been my constant rock in time of need.
We have been married seventeen years, and honey,
I look forward in anticipation for many more to come.
Thanks for allowing me to stretch my wings
and extend out past mediocrity.

To our amazing children Jonathan,
Jennifer, and now Jasmine:
Keep your mind stayed on God
and always have ears to hear what the
voice of God is saying!

Acknowledgments

I would like to acknowledge and thank Keith Carroll, my literary agent, for his constant encouragement and enlightenment. If our paths had never crossed, this book may not have been able to go forth.

To Brian Banashak, my Publisher, and his staff at Gazelle Press for giving me the opportunity and believing in what I'm endeavoring to do through this book.

To my mom (Doris J. Wells) I love you, and thanks for having me.

To Pat Possiel thanks for being a constant friend and always being there to lend a helping hand.

I would also like to thank our children Jonathan and Jennifer who have graciously allowed me to share their struggles of the past, in order to be a blessing to somebody else in their future.

To Jasmine for being such a good baby and allowing me to type over her while she patiently sat in my lap.

To my husband Rolando, on whom I do depend, who helps give me strength to always rise again.

To my Lord, and Savior Jesus Christ for being who He is in my life— apart from Him I can do nothing.

Introduction

There are so many voices that are constantly grab-bing for our attention on a daily basis. Anything from television, magazines, bills, children, phone ringing, family and friends. What does God have to say? Has anyone considered it? If we would be still before God more often, we would be able to hear His still small voice from within.

As you read through these pages I will begin to re-veal the things that can be done on a regular basis to hear the voice of God. If there is any voice that needs to be heard nowadays it's the voice of God!

— *Lisa Banados*

Chapter 1

Be Still

If you will listen diligently to the voice of the Lord your God, being watchful to do all His commandments which I command you this day, the Lord your God will set you high above all the nations of the earth (Deuteronomy 28:1).

Our lives can get extremely busy with working, raising children, paying bills, grocery shopping, and all the other essentials of modern living. There came a time in my busy life when it didn't seem like my prayers were being answered. I would do all the right things, but I didn't feel like I was progressing in any way. Once I slowed down and began to inquire of the

Lord, I finally heard Him speak to me and tell me not to try so hard.

There may be times when we feel like we need to help God out with whatever situation in which we find ourselves. The truth is, He doesn't need our help. As long as we are doing what we are supposed to be doing, the rest will begin to fall into place.

Sometimes we spend time listening intently to the daily news to find out how the stocks are doing or when we should purchase our first home according to the market.

At one point in my life, I had an overwhelming, unquenchable desire to have a home. Everyone that I knew had just bought a home and seemed to be so exuberant and elated about it. I wanted to have that same feeling of satisfaction and comfort of knowing that we owned our own home. To my dismay and outright disappointment, a year after we bought one, my husband received orders to relocate, and we found out that we were going to be moving.

What I had thought would be God blessing us with a home was in actuality my own desire for gratification of my flesh. After we moved out, we always had problems with the tenants we rented it to, and my husband and I reaped a lot of aggravation rather than peace over the property.

Back then, I always assumed that because something was coming our way, and it looked, smelled, and tasted good that it had to be God. Boy, was I wrong. We weren't being still long enough to hear what God had to say about it all. When we chose to do things our way and in our own strength, the results were never good. This is a part of the price we have to pay when we are not focused on Him.

Often when we're making important decisions without asking God or listening to what He has to say about a matter, we get ourselves into trouble. Then we wonder why things don't work out the way we thought they would.

I remember when I had talked my husband into producing a cardio kickboxing video with me. I figured since the doors were opening for us that it had to be the Lord. We were in great shape, and we were living in Hawaii at the time, so how hard could it be to sell a few videos, right? Well, we were able to sell a few copies to some of my students and some family members, but that was about it.

Sometimes we make the assumption that just because we have the faith to believe for something, that God will automatically approve of it. However, we aren't supposed to assume anything, but rather take everything to God in prayer. I had to learn this lesson the hard way. We still have some of those videos in a box somewhere.

If we don't get an answer in the time frame that we want it, then it's a good time to wait and be still. Being still before God, casting all our cares upon Him, and listening to what He has to say in the beginning will help us to avoid a lot of problems down the road. If you think about it, He is all knowing anyway!

> *Pray at all times (on every occasion, in every season) in the Spirit, with all* [manner of] *prayer and entreaty. To that end keep alert and watch with strong purpose and persever-ance, interceding in behalf of all the saints (God's consecrated people)* (Ephesians 6:18).

Nowadays, it doesn't seem as though many people want to take the time to seek or hear the voice of God for themselves. They would rather run into a prayer line and have hands laid on them for prayer or ask someone else what God is saying about their lives, rather than being still before God and finding it out for themselves.

There is a price to be paid when we want to hear the voice of God. It isn't the most popular thing to do either. A person must have the mindset of wanting to hear the voice of God because it won't happen auto-matically.

> *He who has ears to hear, let him be listening and let him consider and perceive and com-prehend by hearing* (Matthew 11:15).

4

When parents talk to their children and ask them to repeat what they have just said, and the children aren't able to do so, it's probably because they weren't actively listening.

When I write music, a lot of it comes from being in the presence of God. At times when I sit down at the table and am ready to write a song, absolutely nothing will come into my mind. However, as soon as I get into the presence of God, my creative juices begin to flow, and the Lord gives me a song in no time at all.

It is important that we know the word of God for ourselves and not be too heavily dependent on others to read and find out things for us. I readily welcome the sweet sounds of my heavenly Father's voice whispering in my ear and telling me of the great and fabulous things He has in store for me.

Nobody can speak wonderful things into our hearts like our heavenly Father can. Even when He corrects us, He puts it in such a way that melts our hearts with His lavish love for us. He holds us with his warm and caring hands so that we only want to do what is pleasing to Him.

One time a believer badly hurt my feelings. I had shared some of the most intimate aspects of my life, and she betrayed me by not being truthful about me. Word got back to me that this individual told other people things that I had never said. It was such a heart wrenching, dark, emotional, and tumultuous time in my life that I wondered how I could ever forgive this person. As tears cascaded down my pillow, and the stench of my own agony sailed through the night and into the morning, God simply said, "This too shall pass."

His words pierced my heart. I quit whimpering, wiped the tearstains from my face, and got out of bed. I remember saying to myself, "What are you doing?" If I had ignored what God was saying, I probably would have stayed in bed much longer and wouldn't have achieved the victory in this area.

God can speak to us at any time of day, and in any kind of way. Even through my whimpering and quiet groans that echoed through the night, God was still able to get a word to me. I was quiet enough in my spirit so that I realized my heavenly Father was turning His sweet face toward me and speaking the exact words I needed to hear so that I could respond correctly.

When we spend quality time with God, we build a relationship with Him so that we will know when He is speaking even if our emotions are running high.

I'm so glad that I know God and His word for myself. I can remember for the longest time when I was first born again, I couldn't figure out who was talking. Was it God, the devil, or myself? That's why it is so important to spend time in prayer and studying God's Word, although it doesn't have to be a long period of time.

I like to wake up first thing early in the morning and pray and study God's Word. Once my day gets started, I find it more difficult to bring myself to a place of being quiet before the Lord and hearing what He has to say. I just seem to do better, and I'm more in tune with His leading when I put time with God first. When I don't, it seems like all "hell" seems to break loose during the day. Things happen such as someone almost runs me off the road, I'm late picking up the children from school, I receive a bad report from a teacher, and/or a large unexpected bill seems to find it's way into my mailbox. Any or all of these things may happen and I am just not prepared to deal with them. At times like this, I feel absolutely inadequate and caught off guard.

> *But seek (aim at and strive after) first of all His kingdom and His righteousness (His way of doing and being right), and then all these things taken together will be given you besides* (Matthew 6:33).

A lot of the times when I am in the presence of God and seeking His face diligently and not what He can do for me with His hands, He'll freely give me answers to things that I was merely thinking about and not wanting to know. We are to go after God's *presence* and not His *presents*. In that place is where the real blessings of God flow.

This past year our son Jonathan was a sophomore, and the school year went pretty well. The year before that was the most trying, miserable, and anguishing time period in our lives. We went through trial after trial. I met with more teachers and counselors than I care to say. That time was a dark, lonely path of desperation for us, but God walked with us through it. It seemed like whatever we had worked for was going down the drain. Every confession that we had made over our children seemed to lay dormant as if the enemy was saying that God's Word was not working. It seemed as though everything that we were praying for was not happening but the direct opposite was showing up in our lives.

Gray, thick clouds hung over our house like a mobile hanging over a baby's crib. No matter how much or how hard I prayed, we still had to walk through it. During the dark, damp nights (damp because of my tearstained cheeks), it felt as if howling winds were beating down our door and the light would never burst on our circumstances. We chose to be still before God, and He eventually showed us the way out of our misery.

Today, we know that the worst darkness always comes before the dawn. At times God will give us answers to things that we were merely thinking about, and at other times, our answers don't come as quickly as we'd like.

Shortly after all those trials that we had gone through had finally ceased, my husband received a $20,000 bonus check. God used all the painful situations with our son's teachers, counselors, and principals for our good, and now everyone knows us and greets us with a smile. I believe God allowed us to go through all that so I could help somebody else make it through their dark, dreary days and give them hope for their tomorrows. We are now able to be a light at that school in the midst of all the darkness.

Sometimes God will allow us to go through rough situations to see if we'll still want to hear His voice and obey what He is saying, even though what we're going through doesn't make any sense at all.

> *If any of you is deficient in wisdom, let him ask of the giving God* [Who gives] *to everyone liberally and ungrudgingly, without reproaching or faultfinding, and it will be given him* (James 1:5).

The natural thing for us to do when we don't know what to do in a given situation is to go to the phone and call a friend, rather than going to God, the One who knows us inside and out. If anybody will know about what to do in a situation or in any difficulty God will!

Everybody seems to have an opinion and many try to give us some advice, and those are not bad things. I'm merely emphasizing the fact that we need to hear the voice of God and learn to trust in Him, so we will know exactly what to do in any given situation.

You may have a few friends now that God is endeavoring to set you apart from or some other thing that God is requiring you to do. When a new season of our life approaches, it may be necessary for us to go to a quiet place with no friends, family, or television, and just seek His face to prepare us for it. With a new season comes preparation for the new responsibilities along with the fresh anointing and empowerment necessary to fulfill them. We must be positioned to receive and hear the voice of God so that we are in tune with His Spirit and His leading. We need to hear what the voice of God is saying so we can receive our instructions and move in the proper direction.

Many of us know that the more we prepare for a trip, the smoother, quieter, and sweeter the vacation usually is. Have you ever tried to take a trip somewhere without a map, simply using your own understanding of the destination because you had been there before? I have, and it wasn't the most pleasant venture either. I remember when our son Jonathan had a basketball game, and I needed to drive him to it. We had given ourselves plenty of time but were forced to drive around for what seemed like hours trying to find the gym and only arrived minutes before the game was to start. We should have gotten specific directions before we set out for the game.

In the same way, God want us to hear His voice so we can make sure that we are on the right path. When we hear the voice of God, we'll be able to know what season we are in, and what we are supposed to be doing. When it is our time to be putting seed in the ground and sowing for the future, we sure don't want to be eating up our seed and then have no harvest.

> *Do not be deceived and deluded and misled; God will not allow Himself to be sneered at (scorned, disdained, or mocked by mere pretensions or professions, or by His precepts being set aside).* [He inevitably deludes himself who attempts to delude God.] *For whatever a man sows, that and that only is what he will reap* (Galatians 6:7).

As long as we are sowing things into our spirit and not to our flesh, we can expect a good harvest. However, if we are doing the exact opposite and not giving God the time to speak into our lives, we need to make a change.

It's time to decide what kind of life we want—a life that is continually blessed by God, or a life that is just hit and miss, lacking all of the benefits for which Jesus died on the cross. Most people would say that they would want the kind of life that is continually blessed of God, but they don't really want to pay the price to have it.

Paying the price is not the most popular thing to do. However, we are not put here to win a popularity contest. Most of us want to do what is pleasing to God because we know that only what we do for Christ will last. Everything else will eventually pass away.

The price might be having less social time for others. For example, there are going to be times when we feel the need to break away from others for a time by not answering the phone or the door. People may start to wonder if everything is okay. (It's when we start doing something different than what everybody else is doing, that people start to wonder about us.)

We need to spend time alone with God when He is taking us up into higher heights and calling us into different terrain. When God is speaking to us and having us move into new arenas, we're really going to have to trust in Him and not lean unto our own understanding.

Taking time out before we begin a new season in our lives can really help us out in the long run. Getting some directions from our heavenly Father before we actually set out on our new adventures can be vital. It may not seem all that important at first, but if we don't do it and then enter some situations and are not sure what to do, we will wish we had spent more time with God beforehand.

And He said to them, be careful what you are hearing. The measure [of thought and study] *you give* [to the truth you hear] *will be the measure* [of virtue and knowledge] *that comes back to you-and more* [besides] *will be given to you who hear* (Mark 4:24).

When we hear a word from God, we can't let anybody or any circumstance deter us from following it. The true test is what we really believe. If we really believe what God is telling us, then we will wait for His perfect timing.

At times things will happen that are totally contrary to what we're believing God for. It is in those times that we really have to press into God's Word and remind ourselves what He has done for us in the past. Then we can more strongly believe that He'll do it again for us in the present and in the future as well.

When it seems like all of heaven is quiet, and nothing at all is happening, we need to be vigilant about staying focused and remembering what God last told us to do. We need to continue to follow His Word and be faithful because He will see us through. We must be still before Him, and then we will realize that He sits on the throne and reigns whether it looks like it or not!

Chapter 2

Tune In

Tuning into to God is still something that I am en-deavoring to do on a daily basis, even in the midst of other activities. It's like when you are standing in the bathroom curling your hair, and you can still hear what is being said on the television set or the radio station.

For example, when we tune into God, He may tell us to take a different route to work or school, without the traffic broadcast advising us to do so. The traffic broadcast usually alerts us of accidents that have al-ready happened. God will alert us of things *before* the destruction actually occurs.

Tune In

One day I had to be at a class that started at 6:30 p.m. God told me to leave a little bit later than what I had planned on. I would normally have left about 6:00 p.m. so that if there was a good amount of traffic, I could still reach my destination on time. I chose to tune in and listen to what the voice of God was telling me, and I left about 6:10 p.m.

When I had gotten on the congested freeway, there was an accident with several banged up cars on the side of the road, not more than a mile away from where I entered. If I had left at the time that I normally did, I probably would have been involved in it. Because the traffic was so heavy, it couldn't have been avoided.

We need to tune in to what the voice of God is saying and adhere to the instructions we receive. I have heard, from time to time, about different incidences when God told people I know to take a different route to their destination, but for whatever reason they didn't follow His directions. The result was that they had gotten into bad accidents (although they eventually came out of it okay). The better way is to not become involved in an accident in the first place. Listening to God's voice can keep us from investing in the wrong stock, keep our children from danger, protect us from unsafe travel, and a myriad of other things. We need to be committed to hearing and obeying the voice of our heavenly Father.

I believe many times God is saying, "If only my children would listen to me,"—kind of how we feel as parents from time to time. We know our children's lives would be so much easier if they would listen to us. Our children would never have to go on restriction, and we would never have to waste our breath, making sure they hear what we are saying. I learned about this first hand. Our son Jonathan is very strong willed and determined. So I knew I had to be just as strong willed and determined to handle him. A parent can't be weak minded and allow the child to walk over them. On the contrary, we as parents need to set the boundaries, and let our children know that no matter what they do, we aren't going to change our mind. When our circumstances in life are trying to get us to react in a certain way contrary to God's word to us, we need to rely on and tune into God so we won't be moved.

When we tune into God and keep our hearts and minds stayed on Him, we will be anchored in peace. The storms of life can be all *around* us, but they don't have to get *inside* us. Once we allow the storms of life to seep in, we begin to sink. However, if we focus on what the word of God has to say, the circumstances of life don't have to take us down. We can be strengthened through adversity if we hold fast to His promises and don't faint.

When I was in prayer one day, the Lord told me to pray for strength for a hardship. At the time, I was thinking to myself *What hardship?* Everything was going fine in our lives as far as our relationships, finances, and health were concerned. I was obedient, however, and started to pray for strength to endure a hardship.

A few weeks later, our finances were severely hit, even though we are tithers and givers. My husband's paycheck was cut in half. The days began to grow darker and soon after not much light could be seen. We held onto God's Word as never before. We began to bite this bullet that seemed to have our names inscribed on it in gold.

There was no other way out, but to look up at where there seemed to be a ray of sunlight showing us where our help would come from. We continued to tithe and give even though some of our bills weren't being paid on time, which was difficult for us. Our testimony had always been that our bills were always paid on time since we began to tithe and give when we were born again 14 years ago.

When I questioned God, He told me that in the end we would have an even greater testimony to which many more people could relate. When we have been through some trials and tests, and have seen God come through for us time and time again, we're able to help others come through on the other side in victory, and not defeat!

Many times we have experienced difficult circumstances and wished someone was able to speak into our lives and be able to relate to us because they too had been through some of the same things. I believe it would have made some journeys a little bit easier for me, if I knew I wasn't the only one going through something. There will be times when we feel lonely, but this is when we can really be strengthened in the Lord and increase our trust and faith in God.

There aren't too many people that want to go through anything just to have a testimony of their own. If I were to have my way, I probably would opt to go without the hardships and suffering as well. It's in these times when the rubber meets the road, that we find out in what, and in whom we really believe. Some people turn away from God when they go through hardships, while others are on their face before God more and more with each passing day.

When I was going through my hardships, I would be on my face before God even more than I was before. I would give more, and I would pray more, and do anything else I could think of. I knew it is always darkest before the dawn, and the devil wants to get us to retreat from serving God.

A hardship for me is anything that we have to endure for a great amount of time. When we were stationed in Ft. Campbell, Kentucky, I remember all the heartache, pain, and suffering that we had to endure. We were always getting into trouble some way or another with some of our neighbors, whether it was something that our son Jonathan had done, or our dog did. It just seemed like whatever we did, we irritated people in some form or fashion. Those were some real trying times for us.

I remember my husband coming home and making comments about his job quite often. His personality is on the quiet side, and he had always been able to leave his problems at the doorstep before he came into the house. However, during this particular time in our lives, we both had some things to say when we arrived home from work. When you both are being tried in the fire at the same time, it seems almost unbearable.

Nevertheless, we stayed steadfast for the most part, and just dug in our heels deeper into the muck and the mire of our despair of unchanging circumstances. When the ground beneath us would begin to be soft and felt like quicksand taking us down for the last time, we would ask God for help and stick out our muddy hands, and He always grabbed ahold of them and brought us out.

To this day, I can remember all the mess that God delivered us out of time and time again. If the devil can see that you don't retreat, and that you tune into God even more than ever before, then the devil is going to get tired of coming around when he can't get a foothold.

It's when you're distracted and are no longer making progress, that the enemy is able to get a stronghold and continues to hang around. That's why we need to guard our hearts and hold on to the Word of God no matter what our circumstances may look like.

We should learn to enjoy the trials and situations that we go through from time to time. These things will only cause us to get stronger in the Lord and make us grow closer to Him, if we allow it to happen. When we get to the place where we really enjoy what we're going through and allow the refining process to take place, we are truly in the place of victory.

What the enemy wants to do is to discourage us and make us feel as if nobody else has ever gone through what we are going through. However, if we really want to tune in and listen to God we can proceed victoriously. We have the choice to do so. We just need to keep our focus on God, and not on what the devil is trying to do to us.

Consider it wholly joyful, my brethren, whenever you are enveloped in, or encounter trials of any sort or fall into various temptations (James 1:2).

All of us will have times when we are up against a challenge. It is in those times when we can be strengthened to endure and come out stronger because of them. Otherwise we will cave in to these tests and trials and they will overwhelm us. I'm sure many of us would rather allow God to use the trial and make us become better and not bitter, but it's a lot easier said than done. However, if we are prepared to do battle on a daily basis, then we shouldn't be caught off guard by what the devil is doing. Our attitude should be "Oh, it's only you" and not, "I'm so tired of the devil being on the attack"!

It's all in the attitude and in keeping ourselves in tune with the voice of God. If we do this, then often the Lord will forewarn us of the things to come and caution us to be on our guard. We are to be living in victory daily. We shouldn't be taking five steps forward and then be knocked back ten steps.

If you're saying to yourself "I don't think I will ever be able to get ahead," begin to change your words, and your attitude. Your attitude determines your altitude. If we have the wrong attitude, the devil is able to bring us down.

Just before we won a car in Hawaii a few years ago, I remember the Lord asked me at the drawing: "Are you ready for this?" I said "Yes, let's do this!" I even cleaned my sunglasses in preparation to go on stage, and the next thing I knew they called my name.

Even though I believed for the blessing in faith, I still screamed like a crazy person that didn't have any self-control. My family ran with exhilaration with me onto the stage, and the announcer was talking about us and the vehicle. I grabbed the microphone with overwhelming excitement and praised God like He was the one giving us the keys.

All we have to do is to change the way we think, and the words that we are speaking, and everything else will fall into place. It's the little things that we are doing daily that determine the direction in which we will be headed. If we aren't tuning in to the voice of God but we're doing our own thing, then we're going to experience the disastrous results of doing so.

At that particular time I was tuned in to what God was telling me, and I believe because I was listening and answered back in faith, God honored it and allowed us to win that vehicle. Otherwise, if we were disobedient children and never cared what God had to say to us, then most assuredly we wouldn't have won anything, not even a free lunch at the local fast food place.

We would be open to more of God's blessing if we were looking for it. Sometimes we need to stop and be still before the Lord, to keep ourselves from getting into trouble. If we think about the times when we get ourselves into some type of mess, it is usually because we weren't doing what the Lord was leading us to do. We may have chosen to ignore the voice of God, take matters into our hands, and do things the way we thought they should have been done.

There have been some situations in my life that have been difficult simply because I chose to override what God was leading me to do. One of them concerned relinquishing our son's disciplinary actions to my husband. My personality type is to be in control, and that was a very difficult and frustrating thing for me to do. Even though I knew it was something that I needed to do, nevertheless it wasn't easy. When I chose to override what God was telling me, things got much worse with our son before it ever got better. We had heated arguments because I wanted to do things my way and in my time. If I held on with a tight grip without letting the rope unravel, I felt that I would be able to hold things together and somehow things would begin to change with our relationship with our son.

Well God allowed me to hold on the way I wanted to, but there was a price that I had to pay for my disobedience. Our son was losing respect for me because I wanted to lead the family. When things got really bad, I finally decided to give my husband the reins. God allowed me to get to the point of despair after handling things the way I wanted. I remember sitting at the end of the stairs with another envelope from Jon's high school. I held my head in my hands and wept like a baby. Tears rolled down my face, and my hair was in disarray because I was scratching the back of my head, trying to figure out what I was doing wrong.

I clearly remember the voice of God asking, "Are you ready now?" I said yes, I couldn't take it any longer. The phone calls coming in from Jon's high school almost daily along with the letters we received were too much for me. This had been going on for most of the school year, and it was exhausting.

All this had happened because I overrode God's voice. Boy, what a nightmare! Shortly after I turned over the reins to my husband and began to be submissive to him, we were back in right standing with our heavenly Father, and all the wrinkles began to be ironed out.

Good understanding wins favor, but the way of the transgressor is hard [like the barren, dry soil or the impassible swamp] (Proverbs 13:15).

I am a witness to the above scripture in Proverbs. I don't want to learn things the hard way if I don't have to. I have learned to tune into the voice of God and adhere to what He is saying, and my life has been the better for doing so.

I can hear parents saying to themselves "If only my children would listen to what I am saying." How do you think our heavenly Father feels when we, His children, aren't listening to Him? It's just like when our children go through a trying situation that they didn't need to go through, if they had only listened to us in the first place. I can hear God saying, "If only my people would take heed to my voice, then they wouldn't be getting themselves into the trouble they have been getting in."

I believe our greatest lessons are learned when we go through difficult situations. If we never had to go through anything, then how would we be able to endure or be strengthened? I try to use every situation, test, and trial to my benefit. It may not feel good at the time, but I know in the long run it will come in handy.

Things that used to bother me don't bother me as much anymore. What would have made me upset a few months ago, is something I hardly notice now. You don't get to that place overnight, though. It comes through trial, error, and time.

People in today's society don't want to go through anything difficult. They see someone who is prospering and doing well, but they usually don't consider what that individual had to go through to get to that place. The journey to prosperity has a lot of twists and turns in it. Very rarely will we experience smooth sailing without any type of ripples in the water.

Tuning in to God is not always the easiest thing to do. The enemy loves to throw different distractions at us to trip us up and cloud our vision. It's important that we keep in mind that this is why all the tests, trials, temptations, and distractions are coming our way.

If we allow God to work His will in our lives, then we know that all these different situations will work out in our favor.

Be assured and understand that the trial and proving of your faith bring out endurance and steadfastness and patience (James 1:3).

It has taken me some time to get to the place where I actually enjoy the tests and trials. However, it's only because I know I will have the opportunity to grow and be more fruitful in many different areas. I like the fact that I am getting stronger as time goes by.

Now if I didn't allow these tests and trials to make me stronger, I would want to throw in the towel and quit and never get strong enough to help somebody else through their tests and trials.

If we allow God to do what He wants to do in our lives and tune into His leading, rather than what we may think we want to do, we will most definitely be able to help others.

A lot of the times when different trials and tribulations come our way, we think that the enemy is just having a field day with us, and we want to be delivered all the time. There have been many situations I wanted to be delivered from, but sometimes the Lord allowed me to stay in them a little bit longer than what I would have liked.

What would we gain if every time we had gotten ourselves into an uncomfortable situation we would always be quickly delivered? I know I wouldn't have learned as much as I have if God immediately bailed me out every time.

It is imperative that we take the time to tune into what God is saying and then follow through with what He is telling us to do. We must remain teachable, tune in, and rely on the voice of God, and then we can't help but succeed.

Chapter 3

Filter and Flush

Throughout any given day we come in contact with many different people with different point of views. They could be anyone such as family members, close friends, co-workers, or bosses. With this in mind, we just can't leave ourselves wide open to receive whatever may be coming down their pipeline. We also have to be careful not to gossip about someone behind their back or stir up some strife.

The Lord will let us know when we should be filtering and flushing parts of any given conversation. I will usually get a flag in my spirit, as to which way this conversation is going. Sometimes it's better just to end it.

Abstain from evil [shrink from it and keep aloof from it] *in whatever form or whatever kind it may be* (1Thessalonians 5:22).

Many of us know that the enemy would love to use our loved ones against us. I would even dare to say he tries the hardest to use those closest to us to trip us up. However, we don't have to fall prey to that tactic. No matter what the enemy throws up against us, we can find that it is just another opportunity to grow and mature in a particular area.

If these obstacles aren't overcome the right way, this same situation will most likely come our way again until it is handled the proper way. It is only then that we can graduate and move on, and not have to go around that same mountain again.

There have been some recurring situations that came my way. Finally it dawned on me that until I had the right response, the right attitude, and the right actions, I would see this same situation appear again and again.

When we first arrived here to California from Hawaii, everything seemed to be just fine. My husband was starting a new job as an Army recruiter and we obtained military housing on Moffett Field. Then my husband started to work very long hours. Beforehand, when my husband was in the infantry, he always was home by 5:00 p.m. and never had to work on the weekends at all. Being a recruiter's wife is an entirely different story. Rolando leaves for work about 8:30 a.m. and returns home approximately 7:00-8:00 p.m. on a good night. I sometimes cried in the evening when it would get late, and I wouldn't be able to have my time with him. Our children were used to him coming home by 5:00 p.m. and being able to go outside and play basketball for a couple of hours with him.

I guess I was so used to my time that I had enjoyed with him previously that it really tore me up inside. As tears streamed down my cheeks, I would tell God, "This is not working."

I was getting tired of having to keep dealing with the same thing with the same result. When we desire to have things change and head into a different direction, we have to do something different ourselves. So what I did was ask God for some help in the area of my attitude. Ever since then, I've been able to handle my husband coming home so late a little bit better.

There would be times where it didn't dawn on me to change my response and actions in order to see the situation change. However, when we get tired enough of going through the same things over and over, we finally become open to hear what the voice of God is trying to tell us.

However, we have to be careful not to filter and

flush the voice of God. Just because what we may be hearing isn't pleasant to our ears, it doesn't mean that it is coming from the enemy. There are times when the Lord wants me to not say anything when I want to give someone a piece of my mind. For example, one time I entered a store and pushed the clothes back on the rack, so I could slide by it without knocking them off. A woman who worked there immediately said, "Don't push the clothes!" Although on an earlier occasion my husband had remarked that she was rude, I saw this as another opportunity for me to grow in this area and apologized to her. I guess she viewed me as a person that was trying to make her work harder, but in all actuality I was trying to make it easier by preventing an overstuffed rack of clothes from falling to the floor.

Now I could have overridden what the voice of God was telling me, but I chose to behave myself. When the Lord is leading us to do something, but we choose to do something else, then we are just going to open the door to the enemy to harass us.

Sometimes we wonder what did we do to get ourselves into a particular situation, and often enough it is because we were disobedient to the voice of God. We need to tune into what the voice of God is saying as we go about our daily lives. When there are so many other voices, we must filter and flush what is unnecessary. If we don't, then the enemy knows that he can throw anything against us, and we will just accept it all.

We usually take the trash out of our house when it needs to be done, rather than let it build up, overflow, and smell up the rest of the house. This is what will happen when someone comes to us with some trash talk, gossip, or rumors and we decide to receive what they are saying in detail.

If we're not careful and don't cut it off, this same situation will continue to present itself, which shows that we need some growth in this area. However, if we can guard our hearts and pay attention to what we hear and say, then chances are we'll pass the test with flying colors.

Recently I have had some people come to me with some trash talk, which seemed innocent at the time, but I knew at once I needed to be guarded and to watch what I said. An individual came to me with some negative information about someone and tried to package it in a way as if to appear to want to help this person. In all actuality, she wanted to see if I would dish up some more dirt for her to indulge in. If you listen to God, He will tell you what people are trying to do before they even do it.

Yes, I like to help people out and be there when I'm needed, but at the same time people have to know that I'm not going to sit there and listen to just anything. If I feel at the time that their viewpoint is wrong, then I will say so, using considerate words. Some people may not know what they are doing until we bring this to their attention.

Through the past couple of years, I have found that people seem to be comfortable coming to me with their problems and situations. I have learned to become a good listener. I used to wonder why I was the one that was always listening and didn't get to talk much.

I believe you have to be anointed to just listen. In my case, I usually have something to say in return. I have recently realized that this is a part of my calling, and to not run away from it, but to embrace it. I finally asked the Lord why everyone was coming to me for advice. I didn't like it at first because I would think to myself that I have things that I want to talk about too but never seemed to have the chance to express them. I felt like I just kept being put into this situation without even trying.

I recently spoke with the Lord and said, "I don't have a degree in Psychology" (as if it would come as a surprise to Him). I began to wonder if He wanted me to get a degree. He let me know that was not His plan and that His anointing and His calling on my life were enough. I wouldn't have minded going back to college again for another degree; I enjoy taking classes. But sometimes the best education we can get is through God Himself. We may not like the experiences that we have to go through, in order for us to get to where we need to be, but they are for our own good.

When we were stationed in Hawaii, I wanted to attend the University of Hawaii. So without hesitation or reservation I applied. I never consulted with God nor asked Him what He thought. I had simultaneously put in an application to attend and submitted an application for financial aid. I was elated to find out that I had been accepted to this fine university. I hadn't received an answer yet from the financial aid office, so I asked my mom for $1000 so I could attend, while I was waiting for an answer from financial aid. I just knew that since this door had opened for me to attend, I most assuredly would be eligible for financial aid.

A crisp letter from this fine esteemed university brought some of the most jolting, disappointing information. I didn't qualify for financial aid, so for the first time in years, I would have to pay full price to go to college.

Needless to say, I had to tell my husband and let my mom know that I didn't qualify. I had to come to grips with the fact that somewhere in all this I missed God. Not only did I have to take myself out of school after the first semester was over, I still had to pay my mom back, and I'm still working on it.

God knows what is best for us. Sometimes we may think we know what is best, or what direction we should be going in, but we have to learn to trust in the Lord.

Lean on, trust in, and be confident in the Lord with all your heart and mind and do not rely on your own insight or understanding (Proverbs 3:5).

This scripture comes in handy especially when we're being trained to follow the leading of the Lord. When He's telling us to filter and flush and not receive what a person is saying, let's trust that He knows what He is talking about.

When we spend time in the Word of God, then we'll know when somebody says something that doesn't line up with it. If we're not spending the time that we need in the Bible, then it will be harder for us to recognize the schemes and plots of the enemy.

When we're familiar with the Word of God, the enemy won't be able to put us in a position of gossiping about a brother or sister in the Lord. If somebody brings a person's faults to our attention, we shouldn't sit there and tear that person down even further; we need to be praying for him/her. We should be praying for the person that brought this to our attention as well. Sometimes people may say that they are sincerely concerned about someone, but when they start sharing gossip in a demeaning way, they show their true colors.

As believers we should be lifting each other up in prayer and letting people know that we are there for them. If each and every one of us did this, then the body of Christ would be more loving, and trusting, as it should be.

Now if the enemy isn't able to find an open door through family or friends, then he will just come to us directly and try to bombard our minds with negative thoughts. We have to know when this is happening so we can filter and flush all of what the enemy is trying to get us to believe.

The enemy wants to get at least a foothold in our lives in order to have something to work with. It is important that we keep the doors closed to keep the enemy out!

Leave no [such] *room or foothold for the devil* [give no opportunity to him] (Ephesians 4:27).

The enemy is constantly looking for a way in, making it imperative that we stand guard and be watchful of his tactics. We can't be ignorant and think that when we continually progress and do well that the enemy is just going to back up and let us succeed with no pressure.

On the contrary, the enemy hates it when we advance in any kind of way. He purposes to get us off track with various distractions. If we do happen to stray somehow, our heavenly Father makes it easy for us to get back on track.

There will always be challenging circumstances that will come our way, we just have to learn how to handle them with the right response and attitude. There may be situations that seem like they're taking us for a rollercoaster ride, but we just need to hold on because they too shall pass. If we can keep in mind that these trials and situations are only temporary, then we're already way ahead.

It is when we begin to think that a particular trial is too much for us and it will never end, that we are set up for failure. We have to filter and flush all negative thoughts and feelings because if we let them go unchecked, then the enemy can suggest just about anything to us.

If we do keep our thoughts and feelings in check, then we don't have to fall prey to the enemy's attacks. We certainly don't want to be vulnerable to the enemy and his schemes. I'm sure we all are striving to be walking in God's perfect plan and will for our lives.

We need to be careful when we receive a bad report, whether it's from a doctor, a lawyer, school teacher, or a statement from an overdue account. The enemy likes to take advantage of this kind of situation, especially if it's unexpected. Sometimes we get used to the enemy attacking from the same direction, and when he changes his strategy, we are caught off guard. We need to be aware of his activity in whatever situation, circumstance, or trial that comes our way.

> *Be well balanced (temperate, sober of mind), be vigilant and cautious at all times; for that enemy of yours, the devil, roams around like a lion roaring* [in fierce hunger], *seeking someone to seize upon and devour* (1 Peter 5:8).

Because the enemy doesn't want us hearing the voice of God, he is continually trying to get us distracted, discouraged, and depressed. If we can keep these distractions down to a minimum by filtering and flushing, it will be much easier to hear the voice of God.

We have to do our part as believers. God is not going to do everything for us. He has given us this authority, and He expects us to use it. If we don't use the authority that has been given us, then we will never become spiritually mature. If we are new believers, God's grace will cover us since we have so much to learn. However, if we have been born again for quite some time and haven't yet learned to take dominion over the working of the enemy in our lives, then we need to ask God for some wisdom in this area.

We can always ask God what we need to filter and flush. Sometimes we let negative things into our lives without even recognizing them. Many times I sense a red flag when somebody is getting ready to say something to me. When we are in contact with certain people, we know in advance that we shouldn't be sharing anything of great value with them.

We have to learn when we are supposed to be receiving something from another and when the enemy is trying to influence these people to point us in the wrong direction. We will learn the difference over time. When I was first born again, I wanted to talk to anybody and everybody about the goodness of God. Over the years, I have learned that we can't open ourselves up to just anybody, because some people can really do some damage to us if we are not on guard against it.

Someone once said that they had a word for me, and when I listened to what they were saying, I didn't have an inner witness to it. In fact, I had a little red flag come up in my spirit when this person was trying to convince me that God was going to use me in a particular way. This person prophesied in a way that would benefit her. In all the years that I have been a believer, I hadn't heard of anything quite like this, so I was unprepared. In my spirit I felt something very foul was trying to happen, and that this person was twisted in her thinking. I filtered and flushed out that mess immediately before any seeds could take root. We really have to be careful about who we allow to speak over us.

It is imperative for us to go on and do the things that God has called us to do. If we live with a bunch of junk in our systems, then when God speaks to us, it will be difficult for us to hear Him. I'm sure God is trying to talk to us more often than what we think, but we are so full of the world's thoughts and feelings that we have no room for His words.

When we get to the place of crying out, "Where is God?", He is probably saying, "I am right here, but you just have too much stuff on your mind." The cares of the world can keep us occupied for quite some time if we let them. Even watching too much news can be detrimental to our spiritual life. Watching the news is just fine if it is done in moderation. We can get ourselves into trouble when we go overboard with reading the newspaper, for example, and don't even care to hear what God is trying to say to us. Sometimes we have to filter and flush some of the things that don't really seem to be all that harmful, such as watching the news, for example, if their reporting on the bad economy tempts us to hold on to our tithes. We can't totally rely on the worldly system and then expect God to show up when we want Him to.

The enemy can influence our lives in various ways. For example, before I was born again, I used to watch soap operas all day long. If you watch that stuff long enough, you may be fooled into thinking that this is how your relationship with your spouse is suppose to be. I used to think that my husband was supposed to come in the door and whisk me off my feet and bring me flowers everyday. If we were to put our spouses or special loved ones in the setting of a soap opera, we would be very disappointed people. Television shows are not reality, and we as believers shouldn't be living according to a fantasy, but by the Word of God.

Stories in soap operas can go on and on, and one woman can be with several different men while she is married to another. Even some contemporary comedy shows can be harmful. We just can't sit down and watch television the way we used to 20 years ago. Now even the cartoons have some adult content hidden in them. Then there's the music. The lyrics are so explicit and dirty, imagine what it is doing to the teenagers that are listening to it on a daily basis. Actually it's not even just the teenagers that are listening to it but the younger generation and their parents as well.

The movie industry is something to beware of too. It is seldom when they'll put out some movies that a whole family can go watch together. However, I am thankful for the good ones, and I am hoping and believing that one day in the near future there will be a Christian Movie Theatre where the Christian community can go and have a selection of movies to choose from that are good and morally sound ones.

There have been times when my family and I have gone to rent a new movie release, but we wouldn't be able to do so because of the standard that we uphold in our household. There have been months where we have desired to go see a movie but didn't because there was nothing appropriate to see. Wouldn't it be nice that whenever we felt like going to watch a good recent movie at the theatres that we could without thinking twice about it?

I believe God is speaking to His people to take on this challenge if only we would continue to listen. If we continue to hear the voice of God, and filter and flush, God will continue to elevate His people into prominent positions of influence.

Let's continue to do the right thing by filtering and flushing out the things that aren't of God so we can really hear what He is saying. God will then be able to trust us and promote us into areas of which we may not have even thought of yet. When God illuminates things in our lives that we need to get rid of, and we obey Him, He will, in turn, do great things for us.

Chapter 4

Renew the Mind

It is imperative that we take the time to renew our minds. One of the ways we can do that is through regularly spending time in His Word, otherwise we are more apt to think and do things the way the world does them. By taking the time to read the Word, we learn how to handle ourselves in any given situation and have victory in every area of our lives. It may sound elementary, but all of us need to continually do so, young or old alike.

I tend to wonder why, at times, it seems like some people who are trying to serve the Lord are living defeated lives. Why are so many of God's people struggling with an illness, or are nearly broke, and their

43

marriages are doing so poorly? I know more single people than I do those who are really happily married. I have befriended some people in the past, who attended the same church that I did, and later on discovered that they obtained a divorce.

Why are so many of God's people dependent on medications? A pill is needed for them to go to sleep, a pill is needed when they awake, and the list goes on. We had some special speakers come into our church and minister one Sunday, and they asked the question, "How many of you aren't able to sleep at night?" A little more than three quarters of our church stood up because they needed prayer for it, and the church has over 8,000 people in attendance.

Perhaps, you may be struggling in one of these particular areas. I'm endeavoring to help you and not condemn you. I am merely using this as an example to get my point across about the importance of studying and renewing the mind to the Word of God.

Do not be conformed to this world (this age), [fashioned after and adapted to its external, superficial customs], *but be transformed (changed) by the* [entire] *renewal of your mind* [by its new ideals and its new attitude], *so that you may prove* [for yourselves] *what is the good and acceptable and perfect will of God, even the thing which is good and accept-*

able and perfect [in His sight for you] (Romans 12:2).

Have you ever noticed how much the enemy fights us on spending time with God? It seems like the phone starts to ring or someone comes to the door just when I am seeking God. I don't think the enemy could be more obvious than that! If the enemy can get us distracted from our time with God, than half the battle is probably already won for him.

Ignoring the phone is easy for me, but when someone is knocking on the door, I'm thinking that it may possibly be important, like a Fed-Ex envelope or a package from UPS. Usually it is something important, and I'll go right back into spending time with God. Sometimes we have to get to the point where we must decide if the phone, a visitor, or your children really need your immediate attention or if the situation can be dealt with a little later. However, I have noticed that I do better when I spend time with the Lord first thing in the morning before my day gets started and I have no interruptions. I know everybody is different, however, I have found that this is what works for me. I feel like that is putting God first in my life.

When I spend time with God first thing in the morning, He'll tell me to pray about certain things or give me certain scriptures that I'll usually need sometime during my day. I don't seem to experience as many struggles because God always give me insight about situations, allowing me to take some preventative measure before they even get started.

> *So too the* [Holy] *Spirit comes to our aid and bears us up in our weakness; for we do not know what prayer to offer nor how to offer it worthily as we ought, but the Spirit Himself goes to meet our supplication and pleads in our behalf with unspeakable yearnings and groanings too deep for utterance* (Romans 8:26).

The more we are familiar with the Word of God, the quicker we'll be able to recognize when the Lord is talking to us through it. The Lord brings to my remembrance scriptures when I am thinking about various situations. I may not be necessarily praying about anything in particular, but the Lord will give me some help anyway without my asking for it. He wants to help us and is concerned about everything in our everyday lives.

Memorizing scripture is another great way to renew your mind. Take a scripture that addresses a particular situation and memorize it. Not only will you have the victory in a particular area, but also you'll already have memorized a portion of God's Word.

When I was younger the church I attended always drilled us about the scriptures. The teacher encouraged us to study God's Word and memorize the scriptures and always made it seem fun and exciting. I looked forward to these classes with intensity and fervency because I wanted to be the person to win the prize. I am a very competitive person and like any type of challenge. Even when I was around seven years old I memorized the books of the Bible with ease, and if I was asked to recite a few consecutively, I could rise to the occasion with no problem whatsoever. In actuality what was happening was the Word was being planted into my spirit, and it's one of the reasons why finding a scripture, when my pastor, Dick Bernal, asks for it, comes so easily.

The same is true with studying God's Word and renewing our mind—the more we do it, the easier it becomes. If we don't renew our mind with God's Word, it is difficult to live the life of abundance. We have to know what is in the Bible before we can actually begin to walk it out. We can't just live our lives by what the preacher says on a Sunday; we have to start digging in the Word for ourselves.

When we study the Bible for ourselves, then we'll have the wisdom, knowledge, and understanding to receive all the blessings that He has made available to us. Doesn't it bother you when you know there is something available to you, but you're unable to attain it? It used to bother me, but not anymore. There would be times when I wanted to be able to spout off the scriptures with the fervency, passion, and accuracy the pastor had when he preached to us. I'm not saying that we need to study like a pastor in order to deliver a fire and brimstone message to a hungry congregation, but we need to study with the same attitude of wanting to know God's Word.

Hearing other people telling me what was in the Bible wasn't satisfying me anymore. I wanted to know for myself. I'm the type that learns better when I have a hands on experience, and I have more confidence and reassurance when I do. Renewing our mind and knowing the Word of God for ourselves are empowering. How many times have we begun to put things together for our children at Christmas time, without the instructions? It can be a frustrating experience. If we read the instructions beforehand, then we probably won't have this problem. Sometimes we think that we can get ahead by listening to someone else's instruction, rather than putting in the time that is necessary to learn for ourselves. If you're having a difficult time getting into the Word and renewing your mind, stick with it and you will be blessed because you did.

We can never go wrong when it comes to renewing our mind in the Word. We don't have to worry about spending too much time in the Word of God or in God's presence. We have to keep a balance of everything else, of course, but I have never heard of anyone who had overdosed on God's Word and His presence and wound up in the "nut house."

We need to draw close to God, and He will do the

same to us. I think at times we spend more time trying to court our possible spouse, or spend time with our friends, rather than seek after the face of God. When we take the time to renew our minds, the Word of God will tell us how to keep our relationships healthy.

When we renew our minds, we'll live our lives with more purpose, instead of going through life adrift on the waves that toss us about. Nowadays, some people are relying too much on the world and what it is dictating to them as to selection of wardrobes, movies, or even type of foods to eat.

However, when we put God first in our lives and renew our minds, we'll know exactly what to wear (or not wear because it's too tight or too short). We'll already know that just because people in the movie industry give a movie "two thumbs up," it doesn't necessarily mean that we need to go and watch it.

This discipline won't happen overnight, but eventually most of the time we'll know just from the previews of a movie whether or not it is good to see, no matter what the movie rating may be. We can't rely on the standards and the ratings of the movie industry— we need to rely on God! My family and I went to the theatre to watch a "Disney" movie (cartoon), and I couldn't believe that one of the cartoon characters used a curse word. My husband and I looked at each other and at our children. This movie was rated G. Now if a movie that is rated G has curse words in it, then where does it leave the other movies and their ratings?

There was a time when our household used to battle over what was an acceptable movie to watch, and what boundaries needed to be set and followed. Even with a renewed mind, there are still going to be some battlefields on which we have to stand our ground. The battlefield all starts in the mind. If the enemy can win there, then he'll be able to get you anywhere. Whatever you think about long enough will be the direction in which you will soon be headed.

> *For as he thinks in his heart, so is he. As one who reckons, he says to you, eat and drink, yet his heart is not with you* [but is grudging the cost] (Proverbs 23:7).

I used to have bouts of depression. I would wake up in a bad attitude and live with it all day, without first trying to figure out why I was feeling this way. I would be grumpy and act like a tired bear that hadn't hibernated for the past two years. There was no real reason or explanation for acting this way. There would be days when I didn't want to get out of my warm bed with its crisp clean sheets and cozy comforter that would sooth my emotions. Some people used food for comfort, and I had done this too.

At that particular time in my life, God was there with me, but He let me get to the place of being sick and tired of my own behavior and cry out to Him for help. He always knows exactly where we're at and what we are struggling with. When I began to renew my mind, I knew deep inside that people with God in their lives aren't supposed to be so depressed and unhappy.

> *For the rest, brethren, whatever is true, whatever is worthy of reverence and is honorable and seemly, whatever is just, whatever is pure, whatever is lovely and lovable, whatever is kind and winsome and gracious, if there is any virtue and excellence, if there is anything worthy of praise, think on and weigh and take account of these things* [fix your minds on them] (Philippians 4:8).

You can always track down your actions by your thought processes. If you don't like the way your actions have been lately, then by all means renew your mind and begin to change your actions. By having your mind renewed, you'll know how you are supposed to act. However, if we allow ourselves to stay in darkness with the shades pulled down, then there is no telling where we might wind up. The mind without Christ is a terrible and warped thing.

Before I met the Lord, I used to get so mad at my husband (boyfriend at the time) that when he would try to drive off in his burgundy 1976 Firebird, I would lay on top of it as if to say I dare you to try to get me off this car! I don't know if that was sheer boldness or stupidity to this day. What was I thinking?

Some of the thoughts that I had back then included the idea that if I let him drive off, he might never come back. This was probably a fear of abandonment. I'm so glad that he didn't leave me hanging, and that he had enough fortitude not to be scared away and decide that I was a crazy woman. I'm thankful to God that he didn't head for the hills.

We've been married now for 17 fabulous years and have three wonderful children. Our marriage is the result of having a renewed mind. If we don't renew our mind, it's easy to find fault and pick apart just about everything our spouse does. The natural tendency for people who are married is to be negative about each other. Another natural tendency is to speak divorce at the first sign of struggle. I wonder how many marriages of God's people may have been saved if they would have listened to the voice of God and been a little more patient. God doesn't move in our time, He moves in His own timing. I'm sure there have been occasions when we tried to pin things on God, and He was thinking, "That wasn't me, that was all you!"

Yes, we should deal with problems that are before us now, or we will be dealing with them again later on in life. When the mind is renewed, we know that we have the victory, so we don't have to live in fear. We don't have to retreat just because our adversary rears his head at us. We don't have to have a cowardly mindset that causes us to ignore the problem because maybe it will all go away. The world's mentality is that if we work enough hours to get that sports car, then maybe we'll be happy. If we get that promotion that is coming up, then certainly we will be fulfilled. If I drink this last drink or smoke this last cigarette, then surely we'll have peace of mind. These are all false substitutes. Only God can give us real satisfaction.

I almost fell into this trap too. When I was in management, I wanted to work all these extra, painfully long hours that seemed to have no end to them in order to get ahead. The more you were able to stay after the normal hours you were scheduled to work, the more they would ask you to do so. You can get sucked into this very easily and without any warning. An employee wants to be looked upon as a team player and be easy to work with, especially if they're hoping to be promoted. Unfortunately that extra mile can turn into two miles. Remember we're supposed to be doing things as unto the Lord and not to men. When we continually renew our minds, then we'll have less tendency to go overboard in putting extra hours in at work in hopes of being promoted. God is the one who promotes.

We should resist the temptation to spiral down this twisting slide that would hurl us into some competition to gain the attention of the CEO of the company. The only attention that we should want to get is from our heavenly Father when He looks down upon us with sheer delight and pleasure because we are pleasing in His sight.

When we're pleasing in God's sight, the rest follows. He'll see to it that we stand out amongst the rest. Promotion comes from Him anyway. Now there is nothing wrong with wanting to do a good job and going the extra mile. It is what God expects us to do. However, it's when we have the wrong heart or the wrong motivation behind doing something, that we can get into trouble. Having the right heart and the proper motivation are some of the requirements for promotion.

We have to be careful not to give way to the pursuits of the world because they can be detrimental. The worldly mentality can filter in, if we aren't careful. Renewing, and washing our mind in the Word of God will help us to steer clear of this trap.

As long as we continue to keep our minds stayed on Jesus and wash them in the Word of God, we'll continue to flourish and prosper the way God has always intended for us to do.

Chapter 5

Face the Facts

We're going to have to face the facts sooner or later—whatever we are sowing into our lives is exactly what we are going to get in return. This could very well be a good thing or bad. Either way we're going to get what we have sown.

This may sound kind of harsh, but hopefully you have been sowing to your spirit instead of your flesh. The difference between sowing to your spirit rather than your flesh is evident in the results that you'll receive in return.

Do not be deceived and deluded and misled;
God will not allow Himself to be sneered at

(scorned, disdained, or mocked by mere pre-tensions or professions, or by His precepts being set aside). [He inevitably deludes himself who attempts to delude God.] *For whatever a man sows, that and that only is what he will reap* (Galatians 6:7).

There was a time, about 15 years ago, before we were born again, that my husband and I used to smoke. We finally made up our minds one year that at the first of the year we were going to stop. Now I don't know if it was because we got tired of smelling like cigarettes, paying out the money for it, or having colds a lot. However, I do believe that God gave us grace to have the mindset to keep our commitment.

I had this friend at the time who used to smoke, and she would always say, "Just wait till something upsets you; you'll be smoking in no time." I'm sure many of us have had a friend that seemed like they were just waiting for us to fail. When this particular friend would say that I would mess up and be smoking in no time, I would always reply, "No, I'm not!" I haven't smoked since, and in the month of February, that same year my husband and I both gave our lives to the Lord. Praise God!

The enemy wants us to fail and sow into our flesh. When the enemy tries to come around and trip us up, we need to say the exact opposite of what he is trying to tell us. We don't have to accept what he is saying.

When we take the time to sow into our spirits, our attitudes and our actions will be right. We will have enough spiritual food to sustain us through any attack the enemy tries to bring against us, but we have to know the Word of God, in order for us to use it effectively.

The opposite is true as well. If we don't take the time to sow into our spirits, then we are more open to the attacks of the enemy. Isn't it more difficult to drive a car that doesn't have any gas? Even if our tank is low, almost on empty, we can have the confidence that we'll make it to our next destination.

However, if our tanks are on full, then most likely we're not too worried about reaching our next destination. If you're a boxer, and you've been training extensively for quite some time, most likely you'll be ready when it is time for the bout to begin. You wouldn't dare step into a ring with a professional boxer if you didn't have enough training, no matter how much money was being offered. Nor should we go into battle not fully armed.

I used these illustrations to make the point of the importance of facing the facts and sowing the right things to get the right return. When we take the time to sow financial seeds, and wait patiently, then we know we will have a financial harvest coming our way. If we sow hatefulness and deceitfulness, then we know that somewhere down the road, these things will begin to show up in our lives.

When sowing seeds for a good harvest, we have to be careful to keep the seeds of doubt and unbelief out of our soil, so that we can have a healthy crop. We have to keep our confessions right too. There was a time not too long ago when the enemy said to me that we weren't going to be able to get larger military housing. He told me that they had overlooked and forgotten about us even though we were having a new baby and our apartment would soon become very tight and uncomfortable.

God was the one that had led me to read a particular newsletter that said that they were going to take the two bedroom apartments, remodel them, and make them into four bedrooms. I knew God would bless us with one of them. When we stand firm in faith, then we know God will bless us no matter what anybody says. We can't be sowing for a financial harvest, and in our next breath say, "I don't know how we're going to make it this month, the paycheck seems a little short." We need to hold on and believe God. He's not limited to a paycheck that we receive every two weeks.

I wonder how many times we have stopped our own blessings with our own words and blamed it on the enemy. Why would we want to open our mouths and spew out something that is contrary to what the

Word of God is saying? I don't believe that this is something that we intentionally do. Sometimes we say things without really thinking. However, if we have the right things inside even when we're not thinking too much about what we are saying, our words will be the right words. This is available to each and every one of us. Our heavenly Father wants us to get to that place because He has so much more for us than what we could ever imagine.

We can't be talking negatively and then be surprised when negative things show up in our lives. However, if some things are happening in our lives, and we know that we have been careful with what we have been saying, then it's time to go into warfare mode.

Death and life are in the power of the tongue, and they who indulge in it shall eat the fruit of it [for death or life] (Proverbs 18:21).

The enemy's goal is to get us discouraged and have us abort the vision before it actually comes to pass. It is imperative when the storms of life come our way to speak the Word of God even more. When we face the facts and know that the enemy doesn't always have to be riding our backs, we'll start doing the things that are necessary to keep him from coming to our door all the time.

Sometimes the enemy begins to come around

more when we're on the brink of a breakthrough. Other times it may be because we have opened the door for the enemy, and he's trying to get a foothold. Sometimes he'll bring up something from way back in the past, and a certain situation that we had dealt with a long time ago may try to present itself again. However, we must not be moved by what we see.

Recently, my husband and I were having breakfast together and making comments about how good the food was that he had cooked. Next thing you know comments were being made about something that had happened a long time ago, and the enemy was trying to creep his way ever so subtly and come between us. In my mind I was thinking, *Oh, devil I see you and the tactic that you're trying to use to take something from the past and link it to the present. It isn't going to work.* In the next minute, I was faced with another opportunity to open my mouth and argue a point, or just let it go. I chose to let it go. Nothing is worth getting into conflict with our spouses or our loved ones. Most likely a blessing is getting ready to knock down our door, and the enemy decided to try and keep it from happening. The enemy may know what our weaknesses are, but it doesn't mean that we have to fall prey to them.

We need to stop the enemy in his tracks and show him the door. We'll have many opportunities to do so too. If we are easily influenced by the enemy, then he will do the same thing time and time again to us. It's always good to take things to the Lord in prayer and seek God as to how we should handle a certain situation that might arrive unexpectedly. God is never caught off guard, even though we may be.

As believers we still have problems and aren't perfect, but we know when we need help and to whom we need to turn for it. It's not that we don't ever fall down and scrape our knee, but when we do, we have to dust ourselves off and keep on pressing towards the mark.

If I were to stay down every time that I have been knocked down, then the boxing announcer would have counted me out a long time ago. God never counts us out, no matter how many times that we mess up. I'm so glad that God never counts me out and am thankful that I always have Him in my corner cheering me on. He's even cheering me on when I forget who I am in Christ. He gives me a little reminder by saying, "You're the champ, you're the victor, now get out there!" After coming out of the corner with God on my side, I begin to think, "God is right!"

Why would I want to believe anything that didn't line up with the Word of God? The enemy likes to take advantage of these times when we have fallen short and have us to believe that we are failures. We have to know who we are in Christ, regardless of the situation or circumstance. When we know who we are in Christ, the enemy won't be able to trick us up with that kind of an attack.

It's time to get wise to the schemes and plots of the enemy. It's time to start putting the enemy in the place where he belongs. He's not supposed to be destroying our lives. He only has this kind of access when we hand it over to him. If we don't give him the opportunity, the enemy won't ever be able to destroy our lives.

We have a covenant with our Lord Jesus Christ, and He protects and guards His people so we don't need to be living in fear at all. As long as we are doing what we are supposed to be doing according to the Word of God and to the best of our ability, then we know things will work out just fine.

> *We are assured and know that* [God being a partner in their labor] *all things work together and are* [fitting into a plan] *for good to and for those who love God and are called according to* [His] *design and purpose* (Romans 8:28).

When we are confident and know who we are in Christ, we'll be bolder and stronger than ever before. When the enemy sees that we are not so apt to quit, he'll stop coming around for a period of time.

We have a choice as to how things go in any given situation or how our day will go when we get up in the morning. We can't let situations and circumstances dictate to us how to feel and respond. On the contrary, we need to let the enemy know that these things will not move us. If we wake up feeling a little depressed, it doesn't mean that we have to remain that way. Speak the Word of God over the day and get on with it in victory.

> *Therefore, my beloved brethren, be firm (steadfast), immovable, always abounding in the work of the Lord* [always being superior, excelling, doing more than enough in the service of the Lord], *knowing and being continually aware that your labor in the Lord is not futile* [it is never wasted or to no purpose] (1 Corinthians 15:58).

We experience many of the attacks we do because the enemy wants us to get our focus away from God and onto the things he is trying to stir up. The enemy wants us to be focused on him and on his attacks because then it is very difficult to go on and accomplish what you set out to do. However, if our focus doesn't waver, it makes it easier to continue in the direction that we were going into prior to the attacks.

We must stay focused on our vision. When we know that we are sowing good seed into good ground and are keeping our focus, our harvest is sure to be a bumper crop. On the other hand if we fall by the wayside every time adversity seems to strike, then it is easier for the enemy to try to get us to abort what we're believing God for.

Where there is no vision [no redemptive revelation of God], *the people perish; but he who keeps the law* [of God, which includes that of man] *—blessed (happy, fortunate, and enviable) is he* (Proverbs 29:18).

The enemy doesn't want us to hear the voice of God nor fulfill God's plans for our lives. The enemy would rather have us in an uproar and living in defeat. Thus, we have to know that we have the victory and then act like it.

The reality is that we have an adversary trying to derail any kind of progress that we might make in our lives. The sooner we come to that realization, the better off we'll be. Just because a person may not believe that they have an enemy, doesn't mean that the enemy is going to just disappear from their lives.

I'm not saying that we should be on the lookout for the enemy 24/7. I'm merely saying that we can't just sit around and be taken advantage of by him. We can either be on the attack or on the defensive. I'd rather be on the attack. I like to catch the enemy off guard rather than have him catch me off guard.

I'd like to see the enemy running every time I get up to go in his direction. I want the enemy to be terrified whenever I get out of bed, and my feet hit the floor. We are supposed to be the ones that have the enemy on the run; he's not supposed to have us on the run.

A boxer doesn't get in the ring with his opponent and shrink away somewhere in the corner. No, the boxer usually goes right up to his opponent's face and puts his hands up in victory, like he already knows that he is going to win. Well we should be the same way because we already know that God has given us the victory!

But thanks be to God, Who gives us the victory [making us conquerors] *through our Lord Jesus Christ* (1 Corinthians 15:57).

When we have an attitude of victory, then we can't help but live our lives in victory. Attitude is everything—your attitude will determine your altitude.

If we allow our minds to wander off, without keeping our thoughts in check, then eventually we'll wind up giving a place for the enemy to enter, knowing that when we give the enemy an inch, he'll try and take up a football field's worth.

We should endeavor to keep the enemy on the outskirts of our lives. We shouldn't allow him to show up whenever he feels like it. The enemy should be afraid to come into our homes, because as soon as we become aware of his stench, we put him back out where he belongs.

If our minds are always focused on the negative situations in our lives, then our thought patterns are going to be ones of defeat. On the other hand, if we know that whatever comes our way, we'll be able to handle it in a victorious manner, than our lives will eventually follow that pattern.

> *I have strength for all things in Christ Who empowers me* [I am ready for anything and equal to anything through Him Who infuses inner strength into me; I am self-sufficient in Christ's sufficiency] (Philippians 4:13).

The fact is we have more to say in how our lives will be lived than what we give ourselves credit for. We have the choice of deciding whether we are going to live a life of excellence or one of mediocrity.

However, there is a price that must be paid in order for us to live the way God has intended for us to live. We have choices to make every single day that will determine our outcome. Let's make the right choices.

> *I call heaven and earth to witness this day against you that I have set before you life and death, the blessings and the curses; therefore choose life that you and your descendants may live* (Deuteronomy 30:19).

When we face the facts that in the end we win and the victory is already ours, then we'll do the things that need to be done in order for us to get there. When we choose life and God's way of doing things, we can expect God to bless us beyond measure.

Chapter 6

Knowing in Your Heart

When we know in our heart who we are and the authority we have, then no devil will be able to stand against us. We will begin to have the confidence and the reassurance that when God is speaking, we are able to hear and know His voice.

For example, when I first started to write, the Lord let me know that He was going to use me mightily in this area. He spoke to me several years ago and said that I would be speaking before people and teaching His Word. Several years ago, when I was a housewife, concentrating on raising our son Jonathan, God spoke to me about these things that seemed so far fetched even He couldn't pull them off. Of course with God all things are possible, and God can do anything that He wants to.

Sometimes when He speaks to us about all these great things He's going to do in our lives, it seems like nothing could be farther from the truth. One day I was washing dishes in a kitchen of a house I didn't own in front of a little window facing the backyard with trees, and the Lord showed me that I would be standing in front of thousands of people, as far as my eyes could see. There have been plenty of times that the Lord has blown my mind, and this was definitely one of them. There has been quite a bit of growth since the Lord told me this. We should never judge something by what it may look like at that moment, because things are subject to change.

> *For our light, momentary affliction (this slight distress of the passing hour) is ever more and more abundantly preparing and producing and achieving for us an everlasting weight of glory* [beyond all measure, excessively sur-passing all comparisons and calculations, a vast and transcendent glory and blessedness never to cease]. (II Corinthians 4:17).

Now that I know in my heart that the Lord has called me to minister through my writing, no devil in hell can tell me otherwise.

When he has brought his own sheep outside,

*he walks on before them, and the sheep follow
him because they know his voice* (John 10:4).

In time you will hear and know the voice of God,
and it will become more familiar to you. The different
ways that He speaks to His people will begin to en-
lighten you. A way to know in your heart that you
have heard the voice of God is by the sense of peace
that He gives you. Not only will you have peace of
mind, but you'll begin to develop a sense of boldness
because you know God's will for your life, and nobody
could ever tell you any different.

Knowing God's will is empowering, and you won't
be so easily tricked into thinking that God doesn't care
for you, and that you're all alone. The enemy often
likes to use this approach and run God's people off into
a ditch somewhere if he's able. The enemy can only do
this if we don't have a clue who we are, and if we don't
know in our heart that God is continually working on
our behalf.

The more time that we spend with the heavenly
Father, the more we'll understand who we are. It is difficult to know who we are if we don't ever spend any
time with God, or any time in His Word. Let me give
you an illustration. If I were never to communicate
with my husband or sit down and talk to him face to
face, we would eventually drift apart because we never
took the time to spend with one another. It is imperative to take the time to sit down with God and allow

Him to speak into our lives. We give our friends time by talking on the phone with them or go out to the malls shopping with them, so why don't we give God that much time, if not more? By taking the time and communicating with my husband, I know exactly what is going on in his life. I have this knowing in my heart that we are going in the same direction because I have taken the time to talk with him. If there are any issues at hand, we'll pray together about it.

Whenever you have prayed about something, and you feel uncomfortable, then you should probably wait on the Lord before you go into action. I've learned that the only time that I take action in any given situation is when I have the peace of God.

And God's peace [shall be yours, that tranquil state of a soul assured of its salvation through Christ, and so fearing nothing from God and being content with its earthly lot of whatever sort that is, that peace] *which transcends all understanding shall garrison and mount guard over your hearts and minds in Christ Jesus* (Philippians 4:7).

Having the peace of God is like having the green light to go forth and do what you had been planning and praying about doing. Whenever I don't have peace about something, it's usually because the Lord knows the outcome of something that I was planning on doing, that in actuality I shouldn't be doing at all. God knows things way ahead of time, so we can trust His leading. He'll never steer you wrong.

God can save us a lot of heartache and trouble if only we would hear and listen to His voice. The more we listen to His voice, the more He'll speak to us. He may be telling us to do something right now, so we should be careful to respond when He is speaking.

Sometimes I'll check myself and see if I'm following God right away or if I'm casually responding without any urgency to what He had told me to do. I have even asked God from time to time "How am I doing?" He'll always respond to me right away, and if I need to make a correction, then I go ahead and make that adjustment.

Jonathan is our first born, who is now 16 years old. He has grown up into a fine young man. However it wasn't without some determination on our part. We need to be as focused on our relationship with our heavenly Father. We have to be determined to clear our minds and wait patiently to hear from Him. I'm so glad God hasn't given up on me. I'm sure God knew way ahead of time that He would have to be patient with me.

Be still and rest in the Lord; wait for him and patiently lean yourself upon him; fret not yourself because of him who prospers in his way, because of the man who brings wicked devices to pass (Psalms 37:7).

Don't be so hard on yourself if you find it difficult to hear the voice of God. When I was first born again, I studied His Word and prayed in the spirit a lot. Even though at that particular time I really didn't know how to hear from God, I knew in my heart that I was going in the right direction, and that I was doing what He wanted me to do. The more I was doing what I knew the Lord wanted me to do, the more I was able to recognize when the Lord was speaking to me. He began to show Himself strong on my behalf because I was so eager to get to know Him.

God won't leave you hanging if He sees you trying. Sometimes it can be discouraging when you don't hear from God the way you think you should, or in the time frame that you have set aside. That's why it's important to wait.

There have been times when I have gone into prayer and was waiting on an answer from God, and He wasn't giving me one. I finally said, "I'll stand here before You, until I get an answer." Shortly thereafter I got an answer, but we can't rush God. He does things in a timely fashion. We can't go into prayer, and say, "Okay God, I have ten minutes to get an answer, and then I have to go." You might as well pray and intercede for someone else in that ten minutes, rather than put God on some type of time crunch.

I have noticed that when I go into prayer with

thanksgiving, not giving God my "things I want list," He begins to tell me all sorts of things without my even asking. When God knows our heart, and where we're coming from, He'll want to give us insightful information so we can be blessed all the days of our lives. That is the kind of God we serve.

When we know in our hearts that God wants to bless us, and that He is for us, then we'll be able to go boldly and reverentially before His throne without any hesitation. I know our children don't think twice about asking us for money, or anything else for that matter. They do know, however, that there is a right way to ask and a right way to approach us. Our children don't say, "Give me some money." They know not to demand anything because they know they will walk away with nothing. Our children know exactly how to ask, and they know if I have the money on me then they can have it. How much more does God want to hear, and answer our prayers!

> *If you then, evil as you are, know how to give good and advantageous gifts to your children, how much more will your Father who is in heaven* [perfect as he is] *give good and advantageous things to those who keep on asking Him!* (Matthew 7:11).

When we know who we are in Christ, then we know as long as we do things God's way, that we'll basically be unstoppable. We have to continue to keep going forward. If the enemy comes around and knocks us back three steps, then let's pray that the Lord will allow us to make that up and even then some.

When we first start living for the Lord, He graces us a lot to do the things that He has called us to do. After a while, He'll back up a little bit so we'll be able to stand on our own. Even when we're standing on our own, the Lord is always there to help and aid us. Our daughter Jasmine is a newborn, and we have to carry her a lot because she isn't able to care for herself. However when she is near the age of one, we'll begin to set her down more and allow her to try to walk.

I believe one of the areas that God really wants His people to grow in is their ability to be able to hear from Him. If He can get His people to the place they need to be, we would have significant influence, more than the people in the world.

Yes, I know we as believers have come a long way. However, I believe we should be in prominent places in the theatres, ballparks, restaurants, and everything else for that matter. I believe God wants to give His people so much more, but He has to be able to trust them as well. That's why it is so important for us to hear His voice and to know in our heart that we are pleasing in His sight. I wonder how many times God wanted to promote His people, but He couldn't be-cause they didn't always hear His voice and obey. We, as believers, can't just hear His voice; we have to follow through with what He is telling us to do.

> *If you will listen diligently to the voice of the Lord your God, being watchful to do all his commandments, which I command you this day, the Lord your God will set you high above all the nations of the earth* (Deuteronomy 28:1).

There is always a reward when you do what you are supposed to be doing, with the right attitude and response. When God tells us to do something, and we fail to respond in a timely manner, then that isn't the right response.

God needs to know that when He tells you to do something, you will do it right away. We could be holding up our own miracles without even knowing it. Sometimes we may think, *Why doesn't God talk to me anymore?* Maybe He isn't saying much right now because we haven't done what He had last told us to do. Perhaps we only obeyed Him in part, and He wants us to follow through with everything that He had said. When God asks us to do something, we can't just do it halfway and expect Him to pour out the full blessing on us. God doesn't work that way.

We certainly don't appreciate it when it takes our children 20 minutes to do something we asked of them. We may need to question ourselves to see if we had made ourselves clear in the first place, or if maybe we didn't stress that we wanted it done right away. If our heavenly Father could get us to respond to His voice with some urgency, there would be no telling how much or how far He can take us. God wants to use vessels that are ready and available.

We need to wait for God to open up the door and be ready to walk right in. We don't have to force anything. It will all come easily. When we know in our hearts that we are pleasing in His sight, and that we have done all that we can do, then we simply need to stand firm until our breakthroughs happen.

God will give us insight as to when the timing for our breakthroughs are. We'll be able to almost smell it in the air. Certain people may get irritated by our presence or almost jealous. People will begin to recognize the anointing that we are carrying on our life. They will recognize the light that shines so bright within us and look at us as if to say "What is it about them, that makes them stand out so much?" That is the Jesus on the inside working on the outside.

A believer should be a little concerned if nobody around them is able to tell if they are a Christian or not. When people ask where we go to church, to me they are showing some interest. Even though they aren't asking us if they could go with us next Sunday, it doesn't mean that they aren't interested at all.

When we know in our heart who we are and walk around with the confidence of the Lord, people are going to want to find out what is going on in our lives. They'll want to know what our secret is. We can tell them, "I'm glad you asked..."

Once they finally begin coming to church, we shouldn't worry about the reason why they are coming. They could be coming to see the special speaker that is coming into town that particular weekend or because they like the choir. Whatever the reason behind their attendance, God knows how to reach them. For example, I had always been asking Jonathan if he talks to his friends about coming to church. His response would be "No, not really." I continued to encourage him to invite his friends to church, and for the longest time it didn't seem like what I was saying was making a difference.

However, I had a knowing in my heart that everything would work out just fine. To my delight, the next thing I knew his friends were asking about church and if they could go with us the next time we headed out. One of his friends even stayed overnight on Saturday so he could go to church with us on Sunday. So regardless of what the circumstances may look like, God will come through for you.

When you know that God will come through for you, that He is working on your behalf, and that He is looking for someone to show Himself strong to, you can know in your heart that He'll be looking just for you. This knowing in your heart will come as you trust the Lord and endure a few things. A lot of things will be done by faith, and then as you see God come through for you time and time again, you will have a knowing in your heart that God is in control and that everything will work out just fine.

Chapter 7

Have Faith in God

Having faith in God and believing in something that we cannot see, taste, smell, hear, or feel is half the battle. The enemy will continue to try to get us to look at things around us, rather than believing and trusting in God. Above all else, the enemy doesn't want us to have faith in God. Everything that we as believers do is based on the fact of having to walk by faith and not by our senses.

Now faith is the assurance (the confirmation, the title deed) of the things [we] hope for, being the proof of things [we] do not see and the conviction of their reality [faith perceiving as real

fact what is not revealed to the senses]
(Hebrews 11:1).

If the enemy can get us to look at our circumstances, then he doesn't have to work that hard to
keep us down. It's only when we keep our eyes on
Jesus regardless of what is happening around us that
the enemy has a hard time pulling off his plan. The
enemy's plan of death and destruction doesn't have to
happen in our lives.

We can live from victory to victory and from faith
to faith, as long as we walk closely with God. Having
faith in God interrupts the enemy's strategies and
causes them to fall by the wayside. We don't have to be
the casualties of warfare if we use the weapons that He
has given us.

> *For the weapons of our warfare are not phys-*
> *ical* [weapons of flesh and blood], *but they are*
> *mighty before God for the overthrow and de-*
> *struction of strongholds* (II Corinthians 10:4).

If we keep trying to fight battles with our flesh,
then we will keep losing just about every time. Some
people may wonder why they may have a few victories
in their lives followed by a series of bad events that
wipe out or at least dim the victories that they had
previously achieved. We have to learn to do things
God's way, because in the long run that is the only way
we can truly win and have long lasting victory.

We have to continue to fight the fight of faith, with consistency on our part. If we're living by faith one day, and the next day we're all down in the dumps because of a report card our children have brought home from school, then we are not truly experiencing victorious living.

Before I became stable in the Lord, I was flying up in the clouds one day and groveling down in the dirt the next. If everything was going well with checks filling our mailbox and calls containing good news coming in, I would have a very good day. However, if I woke up and realized that I had forgotten to dry the clothes that I was going to wear that day, or if our car had a flat tire, or the ATM machine would tell me we didn't have sufficient funds to make a withdrawal, then I would have a really bad day.

If our emotions are running high and our thoughts are going unchecked, we could take ourselves on a roller coaster ride. Up and down we go. Notice I said we *could* take ourselves on a roller coaster ride. A lot of the times we have control over our emotions, but we just choose not to yield to God and have faith in him.

Women can't use the excuse of it being the result of their hormones either. Every time I had a bad attitude or what was called back then a "mood swing," I would use that excuse. Then I discovered that all of this was covered under the blood, and that God wasn't going to let me get away with that behavior anymore. My husband would make me aware of whenever I acted differently at home than how I acted in church. At the time when he was talking to me about it, I truly didn't know what he was talking about until he showed me how I was behaving. Once he showed me how I was acting, my jaw hung open, as if in disbelief that he was actually talking about me, but he was right.

I believe a victory has been achieved when all "hell" is breaking loose in our lives, and no matter what comes our way we choose to not be moved, but trust God to bring us out and make everything work out for our good. That to me is a great victory. If you think a victory is when you never have to go through anything, or you are always bailed out right away when you are in a sticky situation, I think you are mistaken. How are we supposed to grow up and mature in the Lord if our way is always an easy one?

If we were to do the same thing with our children all the time, where would that leave them? They probably wouldn't be able to function too well out there in the real world because we were too busy trying to smooth their way for them, long beyond the appropriate time.

When we have faith in God and are in a sticky situation, we can do whatever it takes to handle it. When we handle situations the way we are supposed to, then we'll start living victorious lives. It's difficult to have victorious lives when our thought process is contrary to what the Word of God says. The way we think from day to day is a precursor of the things that will show up in our lives. If we think that we are failures, and that we'll never make it or get ahead, then most likely that is what will happen. However, if we are saying to ourselves that a particular situation is only temporary, and God will see us through, then that is exactly what we will see happen in our lives.

Again, the lifestyles that we lead have a lot to do with what we want out of life, and the words that we are speaking. Even if all "hell" is breaking loose, we still need to speak words of life over the situation. If we just sit by and let things happen without taking a stand against them, then the enemy will continue to gain new ground in our lives.

Whether things are going right in my life or not, I still choose to speak a positive confession of faith. Eventually things will begin to straighten out.

In order that you may not grow disinterested and become [spiritual] *sluggards, but imitators, behaving, as do those who through faith (by their leaning of the entire personality on God in Christ in absolute trust and confidence in his power, wisdom, and goodness) and by practice of patient endurance and waiting are* [now] *inheriting the promises (Hebrews 6:12).*

It's only when we walk in faith and have patience that we will ever truly receive anything from God. The test and trials that happen when we're standing in faith and waiting on the Lord are the very tools God will use to help us to keep and maintain the things that we are believing God for. How many people do you know received some great things from God, but somehow along the way, lost them? We should make sure that our hearts remain right when we start to see God move mightily on our behalf.

Growing in the fruit of the spirit will help aid us in our walk with the Lord as He entrusts us with different things that He wants us to do for Him. Without growth in the fruit of the spirit, it's like giving a child a power tool, when all he is really ready for is a small hammer. God isn't going to give us something that we can't handle.

> *But the fruit of the* [Holy] *Spirit* [the work which His presence within accomplishes] *is love, joy (gladness), peace, patience (an even temper, forbearance), kindness, goodness (benevolence), faithfulness* (Galatians 5:22).

> *Gentleness (meekness, humility), self-control (self-restraint, continence). Against such things there is no law* [that can bring a charge] (Galatians 5:23).

Sometimes we bring things upon ourselves and say

that it was the blessing of the Lord, when in all actuality it wasn't. There are times when we'll jump out ahead of God, promoting ourselves but thinking that it is His timing for us when it really isn't. I have done this many times, and through trial and error, I have learned to wait on the Lord, and His timing for me, although it isn't always an easy thing to do. Sometimes a person may really feel in their heart that they are doing the right thing, but it's in the wrong season. Learning to recognize His season and timing has been something that God had to teach me to do. I used to think if I had the faith to believe Him for something, then nothing should hold it up. I was my own hold up in my life.

I was way off base when I approached God and asked Him what the problem was when I didn't receive what I had asked for. I'm so glad He didn't say, "It's you!" but let me discover it in His time. When we have been walking with the Lord for quite some time, eventually God is going to start showing us some scriptures about waiting on Him. One of my weaknesses is lack of patience. Once I had some growth in that area, then I had to work on waiting on seasons and timings. I am convinced that there will always be an area where I can use some growth. I don't believe we'll ever "arrive" until we're face to face with our heavenly Father. When we get to heaven, we will no longer be dealing with the flesh, and then we can't help but be perfect. As long as we are dealing with the flesh, we're going to be fighting the good fight of faith.

A few years ago, the Lord gave me a vision of my mom (Doris) coming to church with me. I had been believing for this to happen for quite some time. Whenever she came out to visit, I asked if she wanted to go to church, but for various reasons she never did. After while, I prayed about it and gave it to God. When we moved back to California from Hawaii, we started attending Jubilee Christian Center. I asked her to come one day, and she began to come to church regularly.

To everything there is a season, and a time for every matter or purpose under heaven (Ecclesiastes 3:1).

Think about a farmer going out in the dead of winter and deciding that it was a good time to go ahead and start putting all kinds of seed in the ground. Even though I am not the greatest gardener of all time, I know that winter is not the most opportune time to start planting most seeds. Although there are some things that will grow in this type of weather, there aren't many. And when your family is dependent on the harvest of the crop that is being planted, you need to be sure of your timing or you will lose all your seed. If we keep this in mind, then we will be more careful as to what we are doing, and in what season we are doing it.

If we look at it in this context, then we'll understand that there is a time to plant some seeds, a time to water the seed, a time to see some growth, and then finally a time to harvest. This is a process, and there are no short cuts to having a successful harvest.

We may try and take a short cut, but all it does is prolong us from reaching our destiny. Things take time, faith, patience, and effort on our part. When a farmer plants the seeds, and they turn into crops, he also has to pluck out the weeds and make sure the insects aren't ruining his harvest.

If you were to ask a farmer if the work that he does is easy, I'm sure he would say it's not. I remember when I visited my aunt and uncle and on the weekends we would go out to the area where they had their crops. We picked green beans and other vegetables, and it was hard work. I always enjoyed Sunday afternoon after church sitting down to eat the meal my aunt cooked that included some of the things that we brought from the garden. But I also remembered the labor that we had exerted in the process of harvesting them.

Whenever we want a good harvest, there is going to be some labor involved. We don't have to be afraid of the labor because it is apart of the process. The rewards will come, even though it may seem that it takes a little bit longer than what we had anticipated. A farmer doesn't plant seeds and expect a harvest right away. He knows he has to nurture what he had put in the ground, give it time to bud, and mature. We should view spiritual life in the same way too.

We can never outgive God. If we're going to the right church, then we know whatever seeds we sow are going into good ground. Good seed, sown into good ground, will produce a good harvest. Just like a farmer wouldn't put his seed into dry, damaged ground, we wouldn't sow into a ministry that wasn't good soil.

We should endeavor to have faith in God and His leading. Eventually we'll get to the place where we listen when the Lord speaks and follow what He is telling us. Then we'll find the answers to all the questions that we have been looking for. Everything we'll ever need is found in Him, if only we believe and have faith in God.

Chapter 8

To Know Him Is To Trust Him

When we really know someone, we usually trust them too. It's difficult to go through some things with someone and not build up some trust between the two of you.

> *Lean on, trust in, and be confident in the Lord with all your heart and mind and do not rely on your own insight or understanding* (Proverbs 3:5).

When a couple has been married for quite some time and really has gotten to know one another, they trust each other with everything they have. That's how we need to relate with the Lord. We need to trust Him with our life, family, finances, job, children, and everything else that we possess.

When I first met my husband this was one of the areas that I struggled with. The guys that I had gone out with previously didn't seem to be trustworthy. As a matter of fact, I told myself that I was through with guys, and that I was going to take a break and stay by myself.

Then along came this handsome, sweet, kind, patient, loving, genuine guy into my life at a time when I least expected it. I felt like Cinderella in the fairy tale, and I thought to myself he was too good to be true. I wasn't sure about him, so I decided to test him out. I did things that irritated him and pushed every button that I could think of. I would do things like take extra time curling every strand of hair, and using every hair product that had some type of spray. I went from mousse, to gel, then back to hairspray again. My hair was longer than shoulder length back then, so I took forever, making him wait. Then I put my makeup on ever so carefully and was sure to use every compact and lipstick that I had at my disposal. All the while I was dancing to the radio in the bathroom, and I knew he was out there waiting for me and getting grilled by my mom.

An hour later when I was ready to leave the bathroom, my hair was surrounded by a cloud because of all the hairspray that I had used. I walked out looking like a lion straight out of wild kingdom because I had teased my hair to a frenzy. To my surprise, he remained the same and continued to treat me nicely. Anybody else would probably have been long gone. God knew who and what I needed, when I didn't even know myself!

> *But those who wait for the Lord* [who expect, look for, and hope in Him] *shall change and renew their strength and power; they shall lift their wings and mount up* [close to God] *as* eagles [mount up to the sun]; *they shall run and not be weary, they shall walk and not faint or become tired* (Isaiah 40:31).

I had previously given up on trying to find a nice guy, and I believe through that surrender, God saw fit to give me what I was looking for when I didn't even know it myself. Through all we have gone through together, I both know him and truly trust him now. I couldn't think of a better person I would want to spend the rest of my life with. I truly am a blessed woman.

I don't think you truly trust someone, until you trust him or her with everything. Have you ever had someone tell you to fall backwards, and they would catch you? Many of us know that this most definitely takes an element of trust. I tried doing this with my husband and would always make sure that he was going to catch me.

I would inform him that exactly at the count of "three," I was going to fall back, and that he had better catch me. Well I had tested him a few times to make sure that he was paying attention, before I would try to do it. Then I fell back, and he caught me, and that felt so good, because I trusted him to catch me, and he did.

Now if he hadn't caught me, and I hit the ground, then we would probably have had an issue of trust to deal with. I know this may sound a little trifling, but how many times do we get upset with our spouse about little stuff? How many times do we get into an argument and forget what had started it in the first place?

I remember an argument in our early days of marriage, when I brought up stuff that happened when we were dating that had nothing to do with the situation at hand. We need to to forget about those things and quit bringing them up.

I do not consider, brethren, that I have captured and made it my own [yet]; *but one thing I do* [it is my own aspiration]: *forgetting what lies behind and straining forward to what lies ahead* (Philippians 3:13).

I have always wondered why we do the things that we do. Why do we start bringing up things that had happened so long ago? Is it because we can't remember what we were fighting about, and now we are mad and want to keep the argument going no matter what type of damage that it does? In the middle of an argument, we're not thinking so rationally. At least I know I wasn't back in those days. I just wanted to win and have the last word. Praise God that I'm not anything like what I use to be. However, I still have a ways to go.

How many of us can say that we truly trust God with everything? There have been some areas that I trusted God in, and other areas that I wasn't so sure about. Total and complete trust in God is surrendering all areas of our lives to Him.

Although I am competitive when it comes to sports like volleyball, tennis, and so forth, I have realized that I can't bring the spirit of competition along with me when I'm trying to work things out with my spouse. It just doesn't work that way, and nobody comes out as a winner.

Trusting someone to keep his or her word is an altogether different area. If we can't believe that someone will keep their word, then we don't trust them. Now, there may be a reason why we feel that way, and it is usually because that same person let you down at some point in time. That's why it is important to trust in God—He will never let us down.

And they who know Your name [who have ex-

perience and acquaintance with Your mercy]
*will lean on and confidently put their trust in
You, for You, Lord, have not forsaken those
who seek (inquire of and for) You* [on the authority of God's Word and the right of their ne-
cessity] (Psalms 9:10).

Once our trust in someone is broken, it is difficult,
though not impossible, to bridge the gap. If the relationship is valuable to us, then we'll give the relationship the time it needs to heal.

For if you forgive people their trespasses [their
reckless and willful sins, leaving them, letting
them go, and giving up resentment], *your
heavenly Father will also forgive you*
(Matthew 6:14).

When it comes to our children, we should never
give up on them. The children may be a little way-
ward, but without any kind of support from the parents, where will they end up? The Prodigal Son knew
that he could come back to his parent's house.

I know that this is a difficult question especially for
those parents who are dealing with teenagers or young
adults that may be rebelling and using drugs or doing
other things that they shouldn't.

*Love bears up under anything and everything
that comes, is ever ready to believe the best of*

every person, it's hopes are fadeless under all circumstances, and it endures everything [without weakening] (1 Corinthians 13:7).

I heard a mother on TBN explain that no matter how bad things had gotten with her daughter, she just chose to show the love of God. Now I know when a child is beyond the age of sixteen and not following the rules of the house, the current thought is to kick him out. But when you kick a child out of the house, it doesn't necessarily solve the problems at hand and most likely could escalate them into some other awful arena.

Think of how God deals with His children. Were we already perfect when He first called us out of darkness? No, on the contrary, I know I wasn't, and He didn't kick me to the curb and say that there was no hope for me. I thank God that He is so patient with me. All we have to do is try to follow His example.

Therefore put on God's complete armor, that you may be able to resist and stand your ground on the evil day [of danger], *and, having done all* [the crisis demands], *to stand* [firmly in your place] (Ephesians 6:13).

The enemy wants us to quit, so he can have your family, finances, and your children. Why do you think he is trying so hard? The enemy will use whatever he can to get you so that you're not able to function right.

Don't let the enemy tempt you to quit; hold on, help is on the way. Just think about David and how the giant kept presenting himself day after day for 40 days.

The Philistine came out morning and evening, presenting himself for forty days (1 Samuel 17:16).

Everybody else was afraid of this giant, and he kept taunting them again and again for more than a month. The giant was daring anybody to come forth and fight him, but everybody would only look at him in defeat.

How many of us right now are looking at problems in defeat? Do we see the giants in our lives as too big for God to handle? Or do we see them as more of an opportunity for God to show Himself strong on our behalf.

When we go through a lot of tests and trials, then we are given quite a bit of opportunity to stand up to our giants and slay them. The more giants that we slay, the greater strength we'll have. When God allows some giants to stand before us, then He has already provided the victory.

I don't believe it was the fact that David had picked up the stones that brought him the victory, but the fact that he had the faith to believe that His God would back him up. When we have faith the way David had, we will see our giants hit the ground and fall dead at our feet.

David looked at this Philistine and told him how he was going to be defeated. David may have been small in stature, but he knew and trusted in the God that he served. David wasn't intimidated and stricken with fear. He didn't care what his brothers thought about him or anybody else for that matter.

People may begin to talk about us if we get too far out with our faith. I'm sure God is saying, "If only My children would dare to believe me." David dared to believe, and he was as bold as he wanted to be. He already knew that he would be the victor; he just had to let his opponent know it. If we don't talk to our giants, then they'll start talking to us. At every opportunity we should let the enemy know that we're the victors, and that he is the defeated foe. We have to know that the enemy has it all wrong, and if we trust God, He will back us up every single time that we step out on faith.

I believe God works best when our backs are up against the wall and nobody else can get us out of the situation except for God Himself. When this happens, we know that we have to give God the glory because we know it certainly wasn't a result of our doing. We are taken out of the equation. God works best all by Himself. He doesn't need any help from us. Yes, He needs us to follow what He tells us to do, but that is all.

When we get to the place of knowing God and trusting in Him, the enemy won't have much means of entrance into our lives any longer. When we know that

God is working on our behalf and trust Him with our all, then that place we have in God will be unstoppable.

Let's continue to put the enemy in His place, and keep him under our feet, by believing and trusting in God.

Chapter 9

My Sheep Know My Voice

When you apply all the different ways that I have described in this book to hearing the voice of God, you'll become acquainted with His leading and begin to know His voice.

After I had been saved for a short time and spent some time in the Word and in prayer, I began to recognize His voice. I felt so privileged to hear and recognize His voice and that He wanted to talk to me.

I had been under the assumption that He was far out in the sky somewhere. Boy, was I wrong. He is more present than the person sitting next to you in church. Isn't this an awesome thing?

He wants to get to know you too. Right there where you are. You don't have to be a preacher, a teacher, or in the fivefold ministry, to know God's voice. You can be a housewife, a businessman, a teacher, a steel worker, a janitor, or an engineer, and know God's voice.

It is comforting to know that God doesn't play favorites. We can talk to Him anytime and anywhere. He can even be reached after ten o'clock in the evening. We'll never get a busy signal, and He'll never drop out of our calling area. Our signal will never get lost, and we'll always be able to get through.

When he has brought his own sheep outside, he walks on before them, and the sheep follow him because they know his voice (John 10:4).

Knowing God's voice and recognizing His leading will give us a leg up over the enemy, because whenever the enemy may have a trap set up for us, God will alert us ahead of time so that we don't fall into it.

When we have anticipated the enemy, we're able to keep him under our feet where he belongs. It doesn't hurt to be a couple of steps ahead of him. Let's be on the attack, instead of being attacked.

The thief comes only in order to steal and kill and destroy. I came that they may have and enjoy life, and have it in abundance (to the full, till it overflows) (John 10:10).

When we know that the Lord came to give us the abundant life, we won't settle for anything less. Knowing the voice of God is a part of that abundant life. Being able to hear His voice allows us to know what to invest in, and what not to invest in,. For example, we'll know what neighborhood to move into and where we shouldn't relocate. We will have inside information so we don't keep making the same bad decisions over and over again. We will be able to make good decisions just about every time whenever we know and adhere to the voice of God.

The first couple years my husband and I were married, the decisions that we made weren't so bad. Then we made some decisions that weren't good, even though we were in agreement. But somehow the Lord graced us through those periods and covered us so that we didn't feel the full effect of them.

> *But he gives us more and more grace (power of the Holy Spirit, to meet this evil tendency and all others fully). That is why He says; God sets Himself against the proud and haughty, but gives grace* [continually] *to the lowly (those who are humble enough to receive it)* (James 4:6).

After a while we start thinking that maybe we should consult and wait on the Lord a little bit before we made some decisions. We didn't come to this mindset right away; it took us a few times of making some mistakes that showed us there had to be a better way. Over a process of time and receiving some teaching in this area, we learned that when we have peace about something, it is basically a green light for us to go ahead and do what we had planned to do.

There may be times when you don't think that you can or deserve to hear the voice of God because of what you have done in the past. Regardless of the life that you have led, as long as you seek forgiveness and ask the Lord to take control of your life, then you will be able to hear His voice. When you invite God to come in and take control of your life, He'll do just that. This is nothing to be afraid about either. This is something that we should embrace. It doesn't mean that everything is going to proceed real smooth afterwards and that you won't ever have any bumpy roads. You'll just have to learn to stay steady and know that everything will work out just fine. If you can't hear the voice of God right away, it doesn't mean that He won't ever speak to you.

Don't get discouraged, just keep doing the things that you know you should be doing, and He'll begin to speak to you. You could always ask the Lord to help you be able to recognize when He is speaking to you. Always lift things up in prayer. He wants us to be able to know His voice, more than we want to know His voice.

The more time that we spend with someone, the

better we get to know who they really are and what they are all about. The same thing goes for knowing our heavenly Father. The more we go to church and hear the Word of God, and the more time that we spend in prayer with Him, the more we'll get to know Him. If we follow the things of God, we'll know more about Him and His way of doing things. We'll begin to have His thoughts, more than our own thoughts.

For my thoughts are not your thoughts, neither are your ways my ways, says the Lord (Isaiah 55:8).

When we take the time to do the right thing, then the right thing will happen to us. If we take the time to listen to someone else's problem and help him or her out, the same thing will be done for us. It just seems to work out that way. As we take the focus off ourselves and getting our needs met, we will find out how we can be a blessing to others. As He sees us blessing others, God knows that our heart is in the right place, and that He can trust us with other things as well.

When we know what is expected of us by studying God's Word, we'll know His voice because there will be many times that He will speak to us through His Word. Very seldom do you hear of the Lord talking to someone in an audible voice. Usually it's through a still small internal voice—an inner knowing that we have heard from the Lord.

Whenever you aren't sure if it was the Lord that you have heard from, always turn to the Word of God and see if what was said lines up with it. Sometimes I have asked Him to confirm what I think He has said in His Word.

If I ever heard something, and it didn't come from the Lord, I know it wouldn't line up with the Word of God, and I won't follow it. When we're newly saved, it is difficult to figure out if it is the Lord speaking to us or just our own thoughts or the enemy. By comparing what was said to the Word of God, I was able to discover who I was hearing from. It's a lot easier when we know the Word of God because we'll begin to have an inner witness.

Study and be eager and do your utmost, to present yourself to God approved (tested by trial), a workman who has no cause to be ashamed, correctly analyzing and accurately dividing [rightly handling and skillfully teaching] *the word of truth* (II Timothy 2:15).

If we hear a voice that says "Why don't you go ahead and drive yourself into that wall," you know it's not God because He only thinks good thoughts about you and your future. If you know the scriptures John 10:10, and Jeremiah 29:11, then you know that couldn't be your heavenly Father speaking.

Spend time with God in the Word. It doesn't have

to be hours at a time, it could be spending 15 minutes that you set aside in the morning to spend with the Lord. I think a lot of people want to hear the voice of God, but may feel intimidated when they hear of people they know who wake up before the crack of dawn and spend hours in prayer and the Word.

Everybody is different, and we can't compare ourselves to someone else. What may work for someone else may not work for us. We have to start somewhere, so we should begin with a time period that we feel comfortable with. God isn't up there with a stopwatch looking to see how much time we put in on a daily basis. He just wants to hear from us and be an intrinsic part of our lives.

Don't let other people make you feel uncomfortable because you aren't able to keep up with the habits that they have. This is between you and God. You don't have to spend hours upon hours in prayer to hear from God. You can be faithful with whatever time you set aside.

Because you may not be able to spend a lot of time with Him in the morning, the enemy may try and make you feel guilty because he wants to trip you up as much as he can. That's why it's good to go ahead and get used to talking to Him throughout the day.

God knows if you're a mother of two or three children that are under the age of six that your day is consumed with diapers, cleaning, and folding laundry.

This doesn't surprise God not one bit.

> *Roll your works upon the Lord* [commit and trust them wholly to Him; He will cause your thoughts to become agreeable to His will, and] *so shall your plans be established and succeed* (Proverbs 16:3).

We have to start somewhere and make a commitment to set aside some time to seek the face of God, whether it is for 15 minutes or 30 minutes, as long as we put forth some effort in getting to know the voice of God. We shouldn't let anything hold us back any longer.

> *For everyone who keeps on asking receives; and he who keeps on seeking finds; and to him who keeps on knocking,* [the door] *will be opened (Matthew 7:8).*

As you go forth seeking the face of God, getting to know His voice, and basking in His wonderful presence, you'll find that He was waiting for you all along. He wants to hear from you so desperately, if only you would come.

Chapter 10

He Leads Me
Beside Still Waters

When the Lord leads us in the pathway that we should go, we'll know that we won't wind up shipwrecked on the side of the bank somewhere.

He makes me lie down in [fresh, tender] *green pastures; He leads me beside the still and restful waters* (Psalms 23:2).

It doesn't mean that we'll always go down paths of least resistance. On the contrary, the Lord may have us purposely go through some storms that will allow some of the junk to burn off us. However, we will experience the peace of God when we're going through the storms, if we'll allow it to take place without panicing.

And you shall [earnestly] *remember all the way which the Lord your God led you these forty years in the wilderness, to humble you and to prove you, to know what was in your* [mind and] *heart, whether you would keep His commandments or not* (Deuteronomy 8:2).

The Lord can lead us beside the still waters, but He's not going to force His peace upon us—we have to freely receive it. Sometimes we have to receive God's peace by faith because the storm may be so tumultuous that it can get inside of us if we're not careful. It is so imperative to stay in the Word because if some of the storm gets inside us, the Word of God that already is residing in us will cause it to be thrown right back out.

If we're able to keep the storm out of our spirit, then that storm can never take root inside of us and cause us to sink. When we have storms in our lives, it doesn't mean that we have done anything wrong—we could actually be doing something right. I have found that when I am doing exactly what God wants me to do, sometimes the storms seem to blow more often.

Beloved, do not be amazed and bewildered at the fiery ordeal which is taking place to test your quality, as though something strange (unusual and alien to you and your position) were befalling you (1 Peter 4:12).

Let's face it; if we're not a threat to the enemy then he's not going to be messing with us that often. However, if we're constantly interrupting his plans, then we can expect some opposition. We don't have to be afraid of his attacks either, because we're equipped to handle whatever he throws our way. The sooner we come to this realization, the better.

> *In conclusion, be strong in the Lord* [be empowered through your union with Him]; *draw your strength from Him* [that strength which His boundless might provides] (Ephesians 6:10).

Eventually we shouldn't even be fazed by the enemy's tactics, plots, or plans, even if the enemy launches a major attack against us. It's a great day when the enemy throws an all out attack, and our focus isn't even broken.

Be assured that when you choose to get closer to God, the enemy isn't going to like it. Stay steady in the times of turbulence, and eventually he'll move on to somebody else's house. Until then, try to enjoy the journey. Remember it's not about the destination, but the roads traveled to get there. I used to be so concerned about getting to the next level or the next breakthrough. Now I just enjoy myself right where I'm at.

The enemy doesn't want us to enjoy anything.

That is the whole purpose of the enemy bringing a storm upon us. He wants to get us off track and derailed so that we're discouraged from ever rebuilding. However, as long as we keep our eyes on the Lord and stay focused, we won't have to be too concerned about losing our way.

> *In all your ways know, recognize, and acknowledge Him, and He will direct and make straight and plain your paths* (Proverbs 3:6).

Whenever we choose to keep our eyes on the Lord when we're going through a storm, He will make our paths straight and plain and there shouldn't be any confusion in what direction we should be headed.

When we're confused and aren't sure what steps or direction we should be going in, it's because something has broken our focus. We have allowed the peace of God to be taken from us, and the enemy is trying to give us something that we didn't ask for in return. At that point, we need to take authority over the situation and speak the exact opposite of what the enemy is trying to pawn off on us. We don't have to accept anything that isn't according to the Word of God. If the enemy is knocking on our door, we don't have to let him in.

I used to have a problem saying "No, thank you" to telemarketers. Eventually, I learned to refuse them. Once you've done it a couple of times, it gets a little bit easier. I don't think that it's being rude either; it's just being honest and up-front. I'm not a person that likes to play games and beat around the bush. It's best for everyone if they know where you're coming from, in a tactful manner of course.

When it comes to the enemy, however, I'm not going to be nice about it. I'm going to tell him where to go and how he can get there. He is not the one dictating what is going on in my life. The Lord leads me besides still waters, but the enemy wants to see me slapped up against the rocks somewhere.

Do whatever it takes to keep your inner peace. Don't be so easy to give in to the enemy,put up a fight. If it is difficult for the enemy to steal your peace, then he won't be so apt to come around all the time trying to do so.

Holding onto the peace of God can determine the outcome of a storm. If we're quick to give up and want to get out of the boat before it gets to the other side, then chances are we're going to have to go through that same storm again. We'll have to keep taking that same test until we are able to pass it. I have learned this quite some time ago, and I am so thankful. I used to wonder why I kept going through the same tests and trials, and finally I figured out that I was not passing the ones that had been coming my way.

It's like a cycle that will keep presenting itself, but

maybe in a different form. I'm not saying that God brings the storms, but He'll use that adversity to teach you what you need, if you let Him. If the outcome isn't what the Lord wanted, then He'll allow the enemy to bring it by one more time.

Once I finally realized all that, I buckled down, kept my peace, started to outlast my storms, and began to walk in more victory than defeat. It's all in how you look at things. If you're tired of being under attack, then most likely the enemy is going to wear you out. However, if you realize that you're going to be the stronger for it anyway, then the enemy isn't going to have any more fun when he's coming to your house. The enemy will only keep coming around if he has some kind of entrance into your life. If the enemy has a difficult time trying to penetrate your faith in God, then he's not going to waste too much time on you. If you're constantly being led by the still waters, and not easily distracted, then he won't hang around. The enemy is out always trying to see whose life he can tear up.

Be well balanced (temperate, sober of mind), be vigilant and cautious at all times; for that enemy of yours, the devil, roams around like a lion roaring [in fierce hunger], *seeking someone to seize upon and devour* (1 Peter 5:8).

The enemy doesn't want us to have peace and walk

in victory. If he can get us to second guess whether we have heard from God or not, he'll just keep us running around in circles and prevent us from making any progress.

We'll never be able to fulfill the will of God for our lives, if we can't hear His voice. We should be able to hear and know the voice of God in order for us to fulfill the destiny that God has for us. We have to be totally dependent on Him and nobody else. We need to hear the voice of God for ourselves and be lead by the still waters.

It is imperative to get ahold of God on a daily basis, and hear His voice in order to succeed.

About the Author

Lisa Banados was born in 1966, and was raised in San Jose, California. She and her family have been a part of Jubilee Christian Center since the early 1990s. She is active in her local church having graduated from the G12 School of Leaders, is a member of the choir, cell groups, and overall life of the fellowship.

Lisa Banados is a dynamic and prolific writer, who captivates the very essence of the practicality and necessity of having an ever growing and flourishing relationship with our heavenly Father.

She uses her skills and shares expressions and life experiences to which people in today's society can relate. As she encourages people across the globe to have a more intimate walk with the Lord, causing a profound change in their lives.

Lisa, and her husband Rolando have been married for seventeen years, and have three children Jonathan, Jennifer, and Jasmine.

Contact the author
for speaking engagements by sending an email to:
Rolisban@prodigy.net